Antique & Vintage Clothing

A Guide to
Dating & Valuation of Women's Clothing
1850 to 1940

Diane Snyder-Haug

COLLECTOR BOOKS

Searching for a Publisher?

We are always looking for knowledgeable people considered to be experts within their fields. If you feel that there is a real need for a book on your collectible subject and have a large comprehensive collection, contact Collector Books.

Cover Design: Karen Geary
Book Design: Donna Ballard

On the cover:

Oval portrait, ca. 1889.
Boxed photo, 1915.
Coral silk evening gown, ca. 1914. $330.00.
Black and green wool day dress, ca. 1868. $250.00.
Silk evening chemise dress, ca. 1926. $485.00.

Additional copies of this book may be ordered from:

Collector Books
P.O. Box 3009
Paducah, Kentucky 42002-3009

@ $17.95. Add $2.00 for postage and handling.

Copyright: Diane Snyder-Haug, 1997

Contents

Introduction

1914

"Fashion rules the world, and a most tyrannical mistress she is, compelling people to submit to the most inconvenient things imaginable for fashion's sake. She pinches our feet with tight shoes, or chokes us with a tight neckerchief, or squeezes the breath out of our body by tight lacing. She makes people sit up late by night, when they ought to be in bed; and keeps them in bed in the morning when they ought to be up and doing. She makes it vulgar to wait upon one's self, and genteel to live idle and useless. She makes people visit when they would rather stay at home, eat when they are not hungry, and drink when they are not thirsty. She is a despot of the highest grade, full of intrigue and cunning, and yet, husbands, wives, fathers, mothers, sons and daughters, servants, black and white, voluntarily have become her obedient servants and slaves and vie with one another to see who shall be the most obsequious!"

Godey's Ladies Book

"Fashion is not something that exists in dresses only, fashion is something in the air. It's the wind that blows in the new fashion; you feel it coming, you smell it. Fashion is in the sky, in the street, fashion has to do with ideas, the way we live, what is happening."

Coco Chanel

Women's fashions are more than fabric and beads. In the clothing women wore, we can trace the patterns of a culture, the wants and needs of a society, the economy, the politics and most importantly, how society views women and in turn, how they view themselves. From the oppressive tight corsetting of the Victorian era, to the liberated flapper, from the pampering silks and satins of the Gibson girl, to the dour, practical war years, fashions echo each time as it was experienced.

The collector who loves history will find fashion the closest thing to the people who actually lived through any period. Throughout this book, you will not only see the fashions evolve from one form to another, but also, I hope, you will feel the vitality of the women who wore them — whether they assented to the oppressive or reveled in the liberated.

Even though, more often than not, their voices were silenced by their political and social climates, they speak to us through the clothing they wore.

About the Author

Diane Snyder-Haug has been studying and collecting antique and vintage clothing for over two decades and has worked with historical societies and small museums cataloguing their collections. Currently, she is a dealer and appraiser of antique and vintage clothing.

How To Use This Book

The beginning point of putting a value on an article of clothing is the process of accurately dating the piece. This is also the most challenging aspect of collecting clothes since fashion changes rapidly. A style of dress that is the most up-to-date of the season quickly becomes old-fashioned and is replaced by the latest trend. Although I suggest that the serious clothing collector read a variety of books on the subject of fashion history, I have included here a relatively simple guide for dating women's clothing.

The first step toward identifying the age of a dress is to determine the basic shape of the dress, or as designers call it, the "silhouette." The easiest way to determine the silhouette of a dress is to put the dress on a mannikin or a model. What sometimes appears to be a tight sleeve will suddenly show a decisive peak at the shoulder when worn, or that skirt that looked bustled actually has a train which will be apparent on a model. Dresses that survive without their support structures (crinoline or bustle) often confuse collectors. A bustled dress will have a large gathering of folds or pleats center back and fall unevenly to the floor without its support structure. A dress in need of a crinoline will have a massive gathering of fabric around the waistline and hang clumsily around the model's legs. Find the basic silhouette of your dress and compare it with the photograph at the beginning of each chapter of this book.

Chapters of this book are divided into silhouettes as follows: the Crinoline, the Bustle, the Hour Glass, the Gibson Girl, the Tailored Years, The Flapper, and the Depression Years. Each chapter begins with an antique photograph showing the fashionable silhouette of dresses of this period and a contemporary quote from the period describing the day's fashion. The Common Characteristics section of each chapter is provided as a quick check of widely seen features of most dresses of the period. Does your piece match up? Read on. The chapters then break down the period further with information on when certain styles came in and when they were replaced. Also included is valuable information on clothing construction techniques of the times. Characteristics of day dress are described first. Information on unusual fashions, evening dress and outerwear follows. Use this information as a detective would, to provide clues to help pinpoint the date of your dress within the period.

Determining the exact silhouette of a dress is sometimes impossible when making a purchase in a shop or flea market. The following is a list of clues to look for before you make your purchase. These are general guidelines and by no means indicators of the exact age of your article of clothing since there will often be exceptions to these rules, especially if a dress has been altered.

Fasteners:
   hooks and eyes — common before 1915
   "modern" snaps — common after 1912
   zippers — common after 1935

Elastic in waistband:
   common after 1915

Dressmaker's tags :
   printed on waistband — after 1870
   attached to back of neckline — after 1905

Bodice construction:
   "boning" or metal stays sewn at seams inside bodice — before 1904
   no boning — after 1904

Once a dress is dated, the process of valuation may begin. In the days before ready-wear clothing was the norm, dresses were sewn by individual dressmakers, making it rare to find two exactly matching dresses. This makes valuation more difficult. Valuations of clothing are based on several things: age, condition, quality of construction, design, trimmings, material used, rarity of style, and last, for the collector who will wear her antique clothing, fashionableness. At the end of each chapter is a standard guideline of current price ranges you will find for dresses of each period based on type of fabric and trimmings. Clothing is grouped in two major categories, "everyday dress" and "special occasion dress." "Everyday dress" represents those dresses constructed of common "everyday" fabric such as muslin, cotton and cotton blends, linen, wool, tweed, rayons (in later years), etc., and used for everyday wear. "Special occasion dress" represents dresses constructed from fancy fabrics such as velvet, silk, satin, brocade, damask, lace, etc. These are dresses worn especially for parties, receiving callers, visiting, and other social events. The low end price figure in each category represents the dress in its simplest form and the high end figure represents the most elaborate (i.e., with fine handmade lace, hand embroidery, hand beading, imported fabrics, etc.). Individual photographs of actual clothing of the period identified with retail prices will also provide you an idea about how to value an article of clothing. You will find that age alone is not enough to make a piece valuable. A plain muslin dress of the 1850s will fetch a much lower price than a fancy beaded flapper dress of the 1920s. The general rule: the more elaborate the article of clothing, the more valuable. Of course, dresses made by famous designers or worn by famous women stand in a category of their own. These are not addressed in this book.

Hats and bonnets, parasols, bridal gowns, mourning dresses and sportswear are covered in Chapters 8-10. Price valuations are given and once again, the most elaborate examples bring the high end prices. Dresses surviving with original accessories should never be separated and are generally worth more as a set. Those pictured in this book which are part of a set have prices given as a set.

Clothing is a relatively new field among collectors, and the field is wide open with many potential discoveries still tucked away in attics. The astute collector will find many bargains, but should be aware of unknowledgeable people who may overprice or misrepresent pieces. Misdating of dresses is common, and any collector should be wary of information passed on to him/her at the time of a purchase. I have seen post-World War II dresses with zippers sold as 1920s and marked as such in antique shops. I have talked with descendants who are sure their great-grandmother's wedding dress is from 1875, only to find, upon examination of church records, that great-grandma was actually married in 1889. In working with small museums and historical societies, I have found similarly misdated items among their collections. Recollection of when something was worn is only one clue in pinning a date on dress, and the dress must match up with period style and construction techniques before a definite date can be ascertained.

Price valuation in this book, unless otherwise noted, is based on excellent condition of the garment in question. Since all fabric deteriorates to some extent with time, "excellent" should be interpreted as having no readily noticeable flaws. Rips, tears, stains, holes, missing pieces and poorly made alterations all devalue a garment. Depending on the defect, a garment can be devalued to little or nothing. But don't relegate a garment to the trash bin until you have read the Care and Restoration chapter of this book. Prices in this book reflect general retail prices found at reputable dealers across the Midwestern and Southeastern states.

Chapter I
The Crinoline 1850-1869

Plate 1: The Bell Silhouette. *Silk day dress with bell sleeves, skirt worn over a large cage crinoline. Ca. 1858.*

Common Characteristics

Skirts are gauged, gathered or pleated all around the waistband or waistline in one piece dresses.
Skirts measure from 10 feet to 18 feet around the hem; average skirt measurement is between 12
    and 15 feet at the hem.
Trimmings are minimal, usually flat bands of applied decoration or ruffles, if any.
Hook and eye or fancy buttons used as fasteners.

General Information

The reign of the crinoline, or hoop skirt as it is sometimes called, coincided with the glorious years of the reign of Napoleon III and Empress Eugenie. The fashionable silhouette was the bell shape, the woman's torso rising from a massive bell of a skirt like a stamen from a flower. Empress Eugenie was responsible, in part, for popularizing this fashion worldwide, often sending crinolines as gifts to royalty in Third World countries, although her recipients were not always quite sure what to do with them. In the United States, civil war rang out and women with Confederate sympathies found the crinoline a most handy place under which to smuggle ammunition and contraband goods across the Mason-Dixon Line since, of course, no one would dream of searching under a woman's skirt!

Two events in the 1850s revolutionized women's fashion. The first was the invention of the sewing machine which was first patented in the 1840s and mass-produced in the 1850s so that very few dresses after 1856 are entirely hand-sewn, although hand finishing of finer details is seen into the twentieth century. The second was the invention of the hooped petticoat. Prior to this, women wore as many as 10 petticoats under their skirts to achieve the desired fullness. The first hoops were petticoats with whalebone or cane inserted into them. In 1856, the cage crinoline was invented. This was a clever device made of rings of steel strung together by bands of burlap (see Plate 2). This device allowed skirts to become very large and also very dangerous. Many were the deaths and injuries reported of women who burned when their voluminous skirts were ignited while standing next to an open fireplace or whose skirts prevented them from making a timely escape when a disaster struck. After several such occurrences, Empress Eugenie had the crinoline banned at large court functions in France.

Fabrics of this period were rich and varied. Prints were much worn, and some fabrics had borders printed on them. Lightweight muslins and cottons were very popular along with corded silks and brocades. Aniline dyes were introduced in the 1860s and many of these later dresses were printed in dark, rich colors, such as reddish purple, which were not available earlier. Fringed trimming was seen in the 1850s, and the most typical trimming of the 1860s consisted of bold, geometric lines made with braid or bands of velvet. (See Plate 3.)

Dresses of this period are found in one piece with a rounded or V-shaped waistline or in two pieces with separate skirt and bodice.

Plate 2: *The Cage Crinoline. Burlap straps hold rings of steel. Ca. 1868. Earlier crinolines have steel rings continuing up to the waistband.* **Value: $75.00**

Plate 3: *Corded silk and velvet day dress with peg top coat sleeves, bold geometrical trim. Dress survives with matching casaque jacket, see Plate 12. Ca. 1864. Some staining on skirt and jacket.* **Value of set: mint value, $350.00; as is, $125.00**

The Bodice

Whether the bodice was sewn to the skirt or separate, the most typical bodice of day dress fastened center front with fancy buttons or "invisibly" with hooks and eyes. Before 1860, the bodice with the V-shaped waistline was the most common. After 1860, a rounded waistline was more often seen.

The jacket-style bodice was introduced in the 1850s and became very popular in the 1860s. Many jacket-style bodices hooked at the base of the throat and did not close at the waist. The "polonaise," a jacket with an attached overskirt in princess style, that is, without a waistline, appeared near the end of the 1860s. (See Plates 4 and 15.)

The waistline was at natural level in 1850, but by 1865 it rose to a slightly higher level. These later bodices measure between 14 and 15 inches from shoulder seam to waistline.

In the 1850s, shoulder seams drooped slightly below the shoulder. The most popular sleeve of the 1850s was the bell-shaped sleeve (see Plates 1 and 5). These widened into an open bell at the wrist. Shorter "pagoda sleeves" were also seen; they also widened into a bell shape but ended at the elbow and were worn with separate undersleeves which tied below the elbow. These undersleeves were known as "engageants." The bishop sleeve, with a closed cuff, appeared around 1858 (see Plate 16). The popular "peg top" coat sleeve appeared in 1863. This sleeve was cut like a man's coat, that is, with an inner and outer seam, wider at the shoulder but stiff, without gathers, tapering tight to the wrist (see Plate 3). Epaulettes appeared on the shoulders of some dresses after 1859 and were a common feature of the 1860s.

There was no uniform boning apparent on all dresses of this period, however, the most typical boning seen in the 1850s was long, center front bones on each side of the front opening. Many lightweight materials were not boned at all. In the 1860s, short bones appeared in the center front seams. These protruded from the waistline and ended below the bustline. (See Plate 7.)

The typical 1850s neckline was a V-shape (see Plate 5), the V being filled in by a chemisette, which is a dickey-like undergarment, normally in white or lace. In the 1860s, most necklines closed in a circle around the base of the throat (see Plates 3 and 16). These were sometimes trimmed with white collars that were detachable and often do not survive with the dress.

Plate 4: *Corded cotton polonaise and matching skirt. Bands of braided cord trim skirt hem and polonaise. Back view. Ca. 1869.* **Value: $245.00**

Plate 5: *Day dress of printed muslin. V-neckline, tiered flounces on skirt, bell sleeves. Entirely hand-sewn. Ca. 1853.* **Value: $200.00**

Plate 6: *Typical construction of dress of the 1850s. One piece. Bodice is lined with white muslin. No lining in skirt or sleeves.*

Plate 7: *Typical bodice construction of the 1860s. Four small bones are sewn inside muslin lining center front. Peg top sleeves.*

The Skirt

The bell shape silhouette was most pronounced in the 1850s. Skirts of the 1850s were gathered or gauged, that is with fine little pleats normally hand-sewn and pulled together with a thread (see Plate 8), all around the waistline of the skirt. The crinoline became largest after 1856 with the introduction of the cage crinoline and skirts as wide as 18 feet around the hem were found, although the average skirt hem measurement was still under 15 feet. The crinoline of the 1860s became somewhat more funnel-shaped, with less fullness in the waistline caused by the elimination of so many petticoats required before the invention of the cage crinoline. These skirts were normally not so tightly gathered at the waistline and often larger pleats were seen. In 1865, the crinoline began to flatten in the front, foreshadowing the bustle silhouette of the next period. These skirts retained their fullness around the back of the waistline and normally had two pleats at the front sides. By 1868, skirts that fell smoothly from the waistline in the front, while retaining fullness in the back were seen. (See Plate 9.)

Skirts with tiers of flounces were found in the 1850s (see Plate 5) and some of these had printed borders on each flounce. These were not seen after 1858. Most skirts of the 1850s and early 1860s had a pocket sewn inside the side seam. The plain skirt with geometrical trimming was the most common in the early 1860s (see Plate 3). By the end of the decade, double skirts had become fashionable and these continued in popularity into the next period.

Evening Dress

Evening dress differed from day wear with its lower neckline (see Plate 11). In the 1850s, the neckline was V-shaped, falling off the shoulders for formal wear. Sleeves were straight and short, normally covered by a flounce of lace or bertha (see Plate 10). Skirts did not vary greatly from day skirts in the 1850s, and many dresses of this period had a separate day and evening bodice which shared the same skirt.

By the 1860s, formal evening skirts were normally trained. Many evening skirts were worn double, the overskirt being looped up at the sides. Necklines were still worn off the shoulders or were rounded. Berthas were worn until 1865 when bands of horizontal material replaced them in popularity. Short puffed sleeves appeared in the 1860s and, after 1865, sleeves disappeared altogether and the most fashionable evening gowns had shoulder straps of ribbon with or without a fall of lace over them.

Flowers were a favored trim for evening dress of this period, along with lace and ribbons.

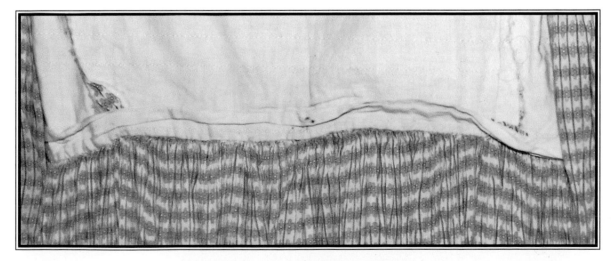

Plate 8: *Close-up of gauging at the waistband.*

Plate 9: *Black and green wool day dress. Front closes with ornate glass jet buttons. Waistline has two pleats center front with gathers at back. Ca. 1868.* **Value: $250.00**

Plate 10: *Evening dress of sheer muslin. Bertha cape closes with cloth flower. Ca. 1860.* **Value:** **$235.00**

Plate 11: *Front view of evening dress without bertha. Rounded neckline suitable for dinner or informal dancing, not low enough for formal ball dress.*

Outerwear

The most popular form of outerwear in this period was the shawl. These were generally long blanket shawls in paisley-type patterns (see Plates 13 and 14). Today, they are often mistaken by dealers and collectors as "piano scarfs" or blankets because of their size. Shawls of this period were normally two yards square or rectangular and measured about 64 inches by 128 inches. The earliest shawls were not reversible; the reversible shawl appeared first in 1865.

Short jackets were much worn during this period, including the "Zouave" jacket which appeared in 1859 with an open front cut away at the waist, and the boxy "casaque" jacket which appeared in 1863 and was usually made to match a dress. (See Plate 12.)

Short circular capes with a seam center back were also popular. These were normally of wool trimmed with braid and lined with silk.

Plate 12: *Side view with casaque jacket.*

Price Valuations

Civil War era dresses fetch the highest prices since they are valued among Civil War re-enactors.

Everyday dresses	$95.00 – 250.00
Special occasion dresses	$250.00 – 400.00
Paisley shawls	$300.00 – 400.00
Capes and jackets	$55.00 – 95.00

Plate 13: *Paisley blanket shawl. Some moth holes. Ca. 1860.* Mint value: $400.00. Value as is: $50.00

Plate 14: *Paisley border shawl. Ca. 1869.* Value: $300.00

Plate 15: *Front view, polonaise and skirt. Large pearl buttons fasten center front. See back view Plate 4.*

Plate 16: *Printed muslin day dress with bishop sleeves. Waistline is higher, shoulder to waistband measures 15 inches. White with blue flowers. Ca. 1865.* **Value:** $165.00

Plate 17: *Simple cotton print day dress, black with white dots. Ca. 1863.* **Value:** $145.00

Chapter II
The Bustle 1870-1889

Plate 18: The Bustle Silhouette. *Two sisters in day dress. Ca. 1886.*

> *"All skirts are drawn so far back as possible, giving an ugly wriggle to a walk, and making sitting down most uncomfortable and often inelegant."*
>
> **Peterson's Magazine**
> **1875**
>
> *"Skirts are made still more clinging, those for full dress elaborately trimmed whilst all street costume seems to be growing plainer. One large pocket is almost always put on the left side, the very tight skirt making it impossible to use a pocket inserted in a dress. All trains are cut narrow and pointed in the middle and where there is a looped up tunic, it is so complicated that it is utterly impossible to describe."*
>
> **Peterson's Magazine**
> **March 1876**

Common Characteristics

Two or three pieces: separate bodice and skirt, or bodice, underskirt and overskirt (sometimes called a tunic).
Use of two or more fabrics.
Use of two or more shades of the same color.
Plain bodice that fastens center front with hook and eyes or buttons.
Decorated skirt.

General Information

The period of the bustle was marked by vibrant social reform movements in England, war in France, and Americans pushing westward and forward with the Industrial Revolution. These were hailed as "modern times," fast paced and exciting. Women's dress reflected this political and economic atmosphere by changing radically and swiftly, so much so that the dress of 1870 bears little resemblance to the dress of 1889.

The bustle appeared in 1870 as a result of the flattening of the crinoline in front and retaining fullness at the back. The first bustles were sometimes worn with a "half crinoline" that held out the hem of the skirt. These early bustles were made of horsehair pads that tied separately around the waist. After 1875 the bustle was sometimes incorporated in the trimmings of the skirt and in the 1880s built-in bustles appeared. The bustle of the first part of the 1870s was wide and rounded at the center back of the waist. Around 1876, the bustle slipped downward until the fullness was centered near the back of the knees. In 1881, the bustle popped back up to the center back of the waist, but in a narrower, shelf-like projection. This odd evolution was attributed to the war in France which briefly stifled the fashion industry. Once France was back on her feet, the bustle re-emerged in its former position.

The most common dress consisted of two or three pieces. A separate jacket-style bodice, the overskirt and the underskirt were most common in this period. Toward the end of the 1880s, the overskirt disappeared and two piece construction was more typical.

Fabrics of the decade were invariably heavy with dresses weighing as much as six pounds. Wools, coarse silks, satins and velvets were the most common. Popular colors tended to be muted and dark. Wines, plums, rust-reds along with dark greens, browns and navy or peacock blues were most popular, although lighter shades and pastels were sometimes seen for summer wear. Dresses made up of two or more contrasting shades of the same or similar colors and different fabrics were common.

Trimmings were relegated mainly to the skirt. Fringes, tassels, large nonfunctional upholstered buttons, bands of velvet, stiff ribbons, bows, and beading (especially jet or black colored glass) were popular.

The Bodice

The center front fastening bodice of the 1860s with a high waistline continued until 1873 when the waistline dropped back to natural waist level. Bodices continued to fasten center front, normally jacket-style with large buttons. After 1874, the waistline dropped even lower and bodices generally became tighter.

Jacket-style bodices normally had tails which fell over the bustle at the back. These were often trimmed with a large bow or ribbons over the bustle. (See Plates 21 and 24.)

The "cuirass" bodice appeared around 1876-1877. This bodice was extremely tight, molded like a corset and often ended in a center point front and back. Both the jacket bodice and cuirass bodices extended well past the hips and were generally not boned. (See Plate 20.)

After 1885, the jacket bodice and the cuirass bodice lost popularity and were replaced with a tight-fitting, boned bodice which ended a little below the natural waist level in a point center front. They normally fastened center front with hooks and eyes or buttons. By 1888, the bodice was back to normal waist level (see Plate 25). This style of bodice survived into the 1890s.

Necklines for day wear were normally high, around the base of the throat, square or V-cut filled in with lace or muslin and sometimes finished with a cascade of lace called a "jabot" (see Plate 22). Around 1874, the standing collar,

also known as the "johnny collar" or "officer's collar" because of its similarity to military styles, appeared and soon became the most popular of this period and would replace all collars for day wear until the next century. These standing collars were normally less than an inch in height. They often had a slit center front and were finished with a ruffle or tiny lace frill. (See Plate 25.)

The coat sleeve, made of two sections, continued in popularity. These sleeves were often of a different fabric from the bodice front (see Plate 19). A brief revival of the pagoda sleeve was seen around 1870. Long sleeves that ended in a large decorative "musketeer" style cuff (see Plate 23) were the most fashionable between 1875-1885; however, plain sleeves without trimmings and tight ¾-length sleeves were seen beginning around 1874. The shoulder seam was back at the normal position. By 1885, all sleeves were worn plain and tight. Beginning in 1887, a slight "kick-up" could be seen at the shoulders in some dresses, foreshadowing the full sleeves of the 1890s. (See Plate 25.)

Plate 19: *Satin and velvet day dress with tie back skirt, simulated overskirt. Jacket bodice buttons center front with upholstered buttons. Early johnny collar is open in front. Ca. 1874.* **Value: $375.00**

Plate 20: *Satin and cotton day dress in three pieces: jacket bodice, overskirt and underskirt. Jacket bodice buttons center front with upholstered buttons. Ca. 1881.* **Value: $285.00**

Plate 21: *Back view. Complicated back drapery of skirt is held in place with elastic bands sewn inside overskirt.*

Plate 22: *Princess gown in three fabrics: corded silk, plain silk and velvet. Fastens center front with upholstered buttons. Lace collar, falling jabot of lace and lace undersleeves are detachable. Ca. 1884.* **Value: $425.00**

Plate 23: *Side view. Note outside pocket and musketeer cuffs.*

Plate 24: *Side view. Bustle with velvet ribbon tails trailing over it. Slight train. Puffing of skirt back is controlled by inside ties. See front view Plate 19.*

Plate 25: *Velvet and satin day dress trimmed with fringes and upholstered buttons. Bodice ends at natural waistline. Kick-up sleeves. Johnny collar. Fastens with hooks and eyes center front. Asymmetrical trimming on skirt. Ca. 1887.* **Value: $395.00**

The Skirt

Throughout the period, skirts were the central focus of the dress, being highly decorated while bodices remained relatively plain.

Skirts of the 1870s and into the early 1880s were most often double skirts, that is consisting of a separate overskirt (sometimes called a "tunic") and underskirt although sometimes the effect of a double skirt was merely simulated by the trimmings (see Plate 19). The underskirt was normally trimmed only at the exposed areas, the overskirt worn draped or looped up to expose the trimmed areas of the underskirt (see Plate 27). Occasionally, the overskirt was still attached to the bodice by a waist seam and this style was called a polonaise (see Plate 4). Some polonaises were so long, extending nearly to the hem of the underskirt, that an unsuspecting collector may mistake them for princess dresses.

Skirts were rarely lined except at the hem with a stiffened "footing" of lining until the end of the 1880s when fully lined skirts appear. (See Plate 28.)

The first skirts of the bustle period were fuller in the front, often requiring the support of a half crinoline to hold out the hem. The bustle itself was worn under the skirt, a separate device of padded horsehair. This early bustle was shaped like a round half-moon. The skirt of this period had many small gathers or pleats that encircled the rear half of the waistband to accommodate the bustle.

Beginning around 1871, the back drapery of the skirt was puffed out, pouched, looped up and in indescribable ways gathered, padded and puffed to give fullness to the rear. (See Plates 21 and 24.)

In 1874, the first "tie back" skirts appeared. These had fabric tapes or ties sewn inside the skirt which, when tied together, would pull the front of the skirt tightly across the hips and upper thighs. Another set of tapes worked at the back of the skirt to control the puffiness of the back drapery (see Plate 28). In the early 1880s, these tapes were sometimes replaced with wide elastic bands that performed the same functions. (See Plate 26.)

The introduction of the tight-fitted cuirass bodice around 1876 necessitated the skirt be worn tight at the hips. The bustle slipped down from the center back of the skirt and was worn near the back of the knees, the skirt flaring from there into a narrow train.

Between 1878 and 1881, skirts were fairly narrow tubes, fitted at the hips with all fullness concentrated center back about knee level (see Plate 107). Shorter skirts for walking, worn two inches from the ground, were introduced in 1878. These sometimes had detachable trains for house wear.

In 1881, the bustle reappeared at the center back. This bustle was less full than the former one, accommodated by just a few pleats or gathers center back (see Plate 29). "Built-in bustles" appeared, consisting of two narrow horizontal steel strips sewn parallel to each other with tapes at the end. Tying the ends together produced the desired bulge (see Plate 33). The bustle began to grow larger, protruding vertically like a shelf.

With the increased size of the bustle, skirts in general became fuller. Between 1885 and 1888, skirts were characterized by their asymmetrical trimmings, i.e., the skirt was draped on one side but not on the other, or this effect was achieved by the use of different fabrics or trimmings (see Plates 30 and 31). The overskirt lost favor and was rarely seen after 1886. By 1887, the previously seen complicated drapery disappeared and most skirts fell smoothly over the bustle at the back.

Bustles began to diminish in size in 1887 and the entire skirt began to become plainer, foreshadowing the undecorated skirts popular in the 1890s. Beginning in 1886, bodices and skirts were sometimes sewn together at the back of the dress but detached in front, or vice versa. (See Plate 32.)

Plate 26: *Inside view of elastic band tie backs in overskirt. Ca. 1881.*

Plate 27: *Underskirt of glazed cotton trimmed only at exposed areas. Ca. 1881.*

Plate 28: *Inside view of tie back skirt. Note muslin footing and hem protector. Ca. 1874.*

Plate 29: *Close-up of narrow bustle adorned with steel buckle. Ca. 1887.*

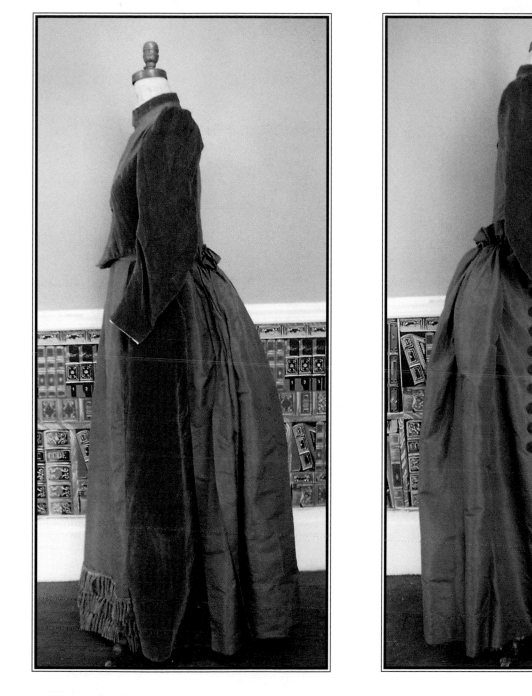

Plates 30 and 31: *Skirt trimmed asymmetrically. Buttons trim one side, velvet fabric panel trims the other. This fashion typical of 1885-1888.* **Note:** *Front view Plate 25.*

Plate 32: *Typical back view from inside: construction late 1880s. Bodice is attached to back of skirt, detached in front. Three bones fan out center back and one at each side. Skirt has built-in bustle.*

Plate 33: *Close-up of built-in bustle. Two steel strips are inserted in the lining with tapes at each end which, when tied together, produce desired bulge.*

The Princess Tea Gown

The princess gown, made of one piece, appeared in the 1870s paralleling the advent of the tight-fitting cuirass bodice. Princess gowns provided a comfortable alternative to the ordinary three piece day dress and were considered "housewear" for occasions such as serving tea in the home. They followed the general styles of day dress, but were worn not so tight-fitting and trimming was not as excessive (see Plate 22). Watteau trains that fell from the shoulders began to be seen in 1877 and continued in popularity into the 1890s.

The Tailor-Made

In the early 1880s, the "tailor-made" dress appeared. These very simple dresses were called "tailor-mades" because the lack of trimmings necessitated expert tailoring by the seamstress. They were worn for casual occasions, sporting activities, trips to the seaside or country outings and were the favored form of dress for working women. Their bodices shared the dominant 1880s silhouette while their skirts were bustled but enjoyed freedom from excess of skirt decoration. (See Plates 34 and 35.)

Evening Dress

Evening dress differed from day dress only by its lower cut neckline; skirts throughout the period were trained for evening wear. The neckline in the 1870s was normally square or V-shaped in front and high in back except for very formal ball gowns when the neckline was low in the back also. Sleeves were very short and plain, or dipped off the shoulders for very formal occasions. Short puffed sleeves that ended at the elbow were sometimes seen in the early 1870s and short sleeves with a slight "kick-up" at the shoulder were seen after 1888. Heart-shaped necklines were popular on evening dress in the 1880s.

In addition to the usual trimmings found on day wear, there was a passion for decorating evening dress with feathers, whole stuffed birds or portions of birds, birds' nests, real butterflies and other small insects. These rarely survive intact on dresses.

Outerwear

The dolman was the most popular form of outwear during the 1870s and 1880s. This was a cross between a cape and a coat, with sleeve openings near the elbow so that the wearer's arms were practically bound to the body. Dolmans were long or short, in very imaginable fabric and often cut shorter in the back to expose the bustle. Capes and mantles were also popular, mantles being capes with shoulder seams. They were normally short, ending above the waist and generally highly decorated with beading. (See Plate 37.)

Price Valuations

Everyday dresses, little or no trim	$85.00 – 150.00
Special occasion dresses, two or more fabrics	$150.00 – 500.00
Capes and mantles, beaded	$85.00 – 400.00
Dolmans	$85.00 – 150.00

Plate 34: *White linen tailor-made. Fastens in front with pearl buttons. Ca. 1885.* **Value:** $100.00

Plate 35: *Tailor-made with matching cape. Green wool. Jacket bodice fastens with steel buttons center front, trimmed with black lace. Cape trimmed with jet beads and feathers. Ca. 1885. Survives with original hat, see Plate 117.* **Value as a set:** $325.00

Plate 36: *Side view, note bustle falls unhampered by excess trimming.*

Plate 37: *Close-up of cape.*

Chapter III
The Hour Glass 1890-1899

Plate 38: The Hour Glass Silhouette: *Full sleeves, tight waist, plain skirt. Woman wearing day dress and mittens, ca. 1892.*

Common Characteristics

Separate skirt and bodice.
Bodice lined and boned at every seam.
Bodice fastens in the front or under the left arm and over the left shoulder with hooks and eyes.
Bodice is decorated while skirt is plain and fitted through the hips.
Sleeves are full but mounted on a lining that fits tight to the arm.

General Information

The "Gay '90s" is a decade which evokes images of barbershop quartets, bicycles-built-for-two, leisurely afternoons passed perhaps playing croquet on the south lawn, and the fervent hum of the woman's suffrage movement. The 1890s was also a decade marred by severe economic depression highlighted by the Panic of '93. The hard times drove many women into the workforce. These women created a demand for "practical" clothing. The bustle was banished and the "New Woman" image appeared — strong, statuesque, yet wasp-waisted, hour glass silhouette wearing a plain tailored skirt and tight-fitted bodice with a high standing collar and full sleeves.

This basic silhouette remained unaltered between 1890-1899. Movement of fashion can be traced, however, in the degree of fullness of the sleeves and the construction of the skirt as the decade progressed.

A NOTE OF CAUTION: *Many dresses between 1904-1910 are similar in general appearance to the 1890s dress and commonly mistaken as such. These dresses also have high standing collars, full sleeves and plain skirts. The difference lies in construction techniques especially the lining, or lack of lining, and the absence of boning in the bodice. See Chapter 4 for more information on this style.*

Fabrics of the first half of the 1890s were stiff and heavy, much like their predecessors in the 1880s. Tweeds and heavy woolens were often seen as well as heavy silks which had been stiffened to rustle when the wearer walked. These rustling fabrics were not seen so much after 1896 as softer materials became more popular. Lightweight cottons, muslins, soft silks, and chiffons were seen as the decade closed with an occasional brocade or plush velvet for winter wear.

Colors of the 1890s ranged from the soft and subdued to bright and bold, with primary colors being favored, especially for trimming. Combinations of colors and/or patterns were typical, some which appear bizarre to our "modern" eye (see Plate 44). Yellow was a favorite color, and "hot pink" was found. As the decade ended, colors tended to become more subdued. Bodices were often highly decorated and typical 1890s trimmings included beading, sequins, folds of fabric, ribbons, and lace. Skirts were plain with trimmings seen only at the hemline, if at all.

Dresses throughout the 1890s, with the exception of the princess gown or the rare tea gown, consisted of two pieces: the separate skirt and bodice.

Plate 39: *Tweed walking dress with ribbon and lace trim, ca. 1892-93. Standing collar measures ½" high and is typical of "lower" collars of the early 1890s. Moderate leg of mutton sleeves.* **Value: $150.00**

Plate 40: *Typical bodice construction of 1890s. Back view.*

The Bodice

Bodices were worn much in the style of bodices seen at the end of the 1880s. Many still ended in a point center front and often center back as well. Round waisted bodices became more fashionable as the decade progressed. All bodices ended at the natural waistline and were worn over the waistband of the skirt, usually fastening to the back of the skirt waistband with hooks and eyes.

Bodices were thoroughly lined and boned at every seam (see Plate 40). They generally fastened at center front until 1892, when bodices which fastened at the left shoulder and under the left arm appeared. These later bodices usually had a lining which fastened separately center front. During the first half of the decade, bodices fit smooth across the bosom as they did in the late 1880s. Beginning in 1894, bodices gradually became fuller, though were still mounted on a tight-fitted, fully-boned lining. The pouched front (see Plate 41) introduced in the 1880s continued to be worn and became looser toward the end of the decade. This bodice style had a piece of contrasting fabric that pouched out center front, although the bodice remained tight underneath this trimming. Bodice trimming was varied and imaginative throughout the decade and bodices became more decorated as the decade progressed.

Standing collars early in the decade fastened center front and were often shorter than later collars (see Plate 39). These collars grew higher and tighter until they commonly reached 2 inches or more in height by the middle of the decade (see Plates 41 and 44). At mid-decade, most collars were smooth at the throat, wrapping around the neck and fastening separately from the bodice at center back. These collars sometimes had a decorative bow or standing fan of fabric or lace at the back, the latter known as the "medici" collar (see Plate 42). Collars made up of soft folds of fabric were also seen.

The sleeve with a "kick-up" at the shoulder (see Plate 43) first appeared around 1888 and was fashionable during the first few years of the 1890s. These sleeves were tightly-fitted and the shoulders rose into sharp peaks. Softer, fuller sleeves appeared between 1891-92 (see Plate 39). Gradually sleeves became larger until they reached tremendous widths around 1895 (see Plate 44). These large mid-1890s sleeves were often stuffed with stiff netting, or glazed cotton to retain their fullness or were sometimes held up with wires known as "sleeve crinolines." These very full sleeves vanished from fashionable dress in 1897. The two predominant forms of sleeve in the mid-1890s were the "leg of mutton" sleeve and the puffed (sometimes called "balloon") sleeve. The leg of mutton sleeve gradually tapered in fullness to the wrist (see Plates 39 and 41), whereas the puffed sleeve ended abruptly somewhere near the elbow and, in day wear, tightened between the elbow and the wrist (see Plates 44 and 47). All full sleeve styles of the 1890s were mounted on a lining which fit tightly to the arm. After 1896, a sleeve with a slight fullness at the shoulder was seen, not unlike sleeves of 1889-1892, but the effect was softer and not so peaked (see Plate 41). The bishop sleeve, a tubular sleeve of the same degree of fullness from shoulder to wrist, also appeared after 1896 and would survive into the next century. From 1898 to 1899, relatively tight sleeves appeared, retaining some type of shoulder trimming such as ruffles or epaulettes. A form of deflated puff was also seen between 1897-1898 which looked like the former puffed sleeve that had been caught up in a stitch underneath and left to hang limply without support.

Plate 41: *Brocade day dress, ca. 1897, with contrasting sheer pouched front trimmed with floral beaded applique, lace at collar and green velvet and lace standing fan or "medici" collar. Epaulettes over shoulders also trimmed with beaded applique. Leg of mutton sleeves. Collar stands 2 inches high.* **Value: $425.00**

Plate 42: *Close-up of standing fan or "medici" collar.*

Plate 43: *Cotton print day dress, ca. 1891. Ruffled neckline extends to cover front fastening. Black velvet trims the cuff. Good example of "kick-up" sleeves. Missing original high standing collar.* **Value as is: $95.00**

Plate 44: *Green and white striped day dress with large puffed sleeves, ca. 1895. Black satin bodice, trimmed with lace and black satin rosettes, pink velvet collar measures 3" high. Cotton skirt is lined with stiff netting, velvet hem protector sewn inside hem. Sleeves are stuffed with netting.* **Value: $375.00**

The Skirt

All skirts during the 1890s were plain, heavily lined and gored to the waistband, that is, made up of panels of fabric which were narrow at the top, widened at the bottom and were sewn together and attached to the waistband without fullness. This new technique in dressmaking allowed skirts to be worn smoothly over the hips without sacrificing fullness at the hem. All skirts fastened center back with hooks and eyes, and had gathers or pleats on each side of the opening to provide slight back fullness. Skirts were worn just brushing the ground and often had braided or velvet "hem protectors" sewn just inside the hem or a 10-15 inch border of stiff muslin, called a "footing," to protect the hem from wear. Linings at the beginning of the decade were generally of stiff fabric such as glazed cotton, although a stiff net lining was sometimes found. After 1896, linings of softer fabrics, such as silk, were more typical.

Skirts from 1890-1893 were relatively narrow, cut with very few gores and fitted with darts at the waist. As sleeves became larger, skirts became fuller. After 1893, "wings" (triangles of fabric) were found in the side seams in the lowest part of the skirt to provide extra fullness at the hem. Between 1893 and 1896 skirts measured as much as 5½ yards around the hem. Some skirts of this period had as many as 11 gores. Skirts with slight trains appeared in afternoon wear beginning in 1895, though most day dress was worn walking length. After 1896, skirts tightened from waist to hip then widened below the knees to produce a bell-shaped flare around the hem. These skirts were normally cut with five gores or less. Yoked skirts were seen beginning in 1897, the "yoke" ending at the knees. These sometimes ended in a "sunray" of accordion pleats.

The Princess Gown

Not as common as the two piece day dress, the Princess Gown was a one piece gown sometimes worn in the 1890s. These gowns echoed all characteristics of regular day dress with the exception that the bodice and skirt were attached at the waistband.

The Tailor-Made

The "tailor-made" separate jacket and skirt popular in the 1880s continued to be worn into the next century. Tailor-mades of the 1890s can be dated by their sleeves which follow the style of sleeves of regular day dress. Tailor-made jackets were seen in a more masculine form than in the 1880s, with lapels and front buttons not unlike men's jackets and were often worn open with a white blouse underneath.

Evening Dress

Bodices for evening dress were cut very much the same way as day dress except with a low neckline. In addition to the typical front fastening, they sometimes fastened center back. Until 1893, a square or V-shaped neckline was seen (see Plate 49). These were normally cut high at the back. Beginning in 1894, curved necklines dipped low off the shoulder and became even lower after 1897. No sleeves, just shoulder straps were common until 1892. Short puffed sleeves ending at the elbow or above were introduced in 1892 and remained for the rest of the decade (see Plate 49). The very large "balloon" puffed sleeve (see Plate 45) appeared about 1894 in evening dress where it tested the water before being introduced into day dress in 1895. Long sleeves appeared in some evening dresses later in the decade.

Evening skirts followed the same lines as day skirts, and for formal evening wear were generally trained, some measuring 18 feet around the hem. The double skirt with a separate overskirt was sometimes seen before 1894 (see Plate 49). Some skirts of this period survive with interchangeable bodices, one for day wear and one for evening wear.

Beading, embroidery and lace were the favored trim for evening wear, although some very simple evening dresses without trimmings were seen in the first part of the decade. (See Plate 45.)

Plate 45: *Evening dress, for dinner wear, ca. 1894. Yellow silk with large puffed "balloon" sleeves stuffed with netting. No trimmings. This dress survives with matching corset.* **Value as a set: $195.00**

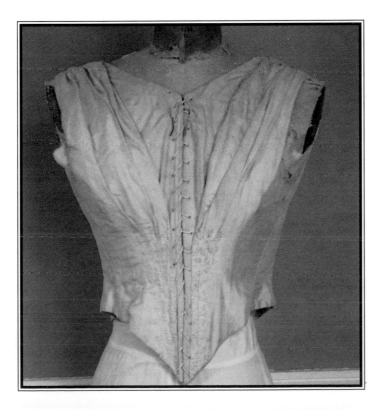

Plate 46: *Matching corset.*

Tea Gowns

Tea gowns were fashionable among the avant garde communities in the 1890s. These one piece gowns were worn for afternoon tea. They generally followed fashionable sleeve styles for daytime, with a neckline which was low in front, but high in back. Watteau trains which fell from the shoulders were a typical feature. Tea gowns of the 1890s are very beautiful, rare finds and prized among collectors. (See Plate 47.)

Outerwear

Until 1895 when sleeves grew to enormous widths, the most typical form of outer wear was the fitted ¾" length coat. These coats had sleeves similar to sleeves on day dresses (see Plate 50). In 1895, the large sleeves made coats impractical and the most popular form of outerwear became the cape. Capes of the 1890s most often had a high standing collar at the back. Velvets and wools, with applied decorations or bold embroidery, were most often seen in coats and capes of the 1890s, and fur trimming was common on coats.

Price Valuations

Bodices without skirts, plain or elegant	$45.00 – 95.00
Everyday dresses, little or no trim	$95.00 – 125.00
Everyday dresses, elegant trim	$125.00 – 325.00
Special occasion dresses, little or no trim	$125.00 – 300.00
Special occasion dresses, elegant trim	$325.00 – 800.00
Tea gowns with Watteau train	$400.00 – 600.00
Coats and capes	$200.00 – 500.00

Plate 47: *Tea gown with Watteau train, ca. 1894. Cotton print, lilies on mauve background. Satin bodice front and collar, lace undersleeves.* **Value: $500.00**

Plate 48: *Side view of Watteau train.*

Plate 49: *Formal ball gown with train, gold damask, sheer hand embroidered overskirt, ca. 1892. Underskirt of gold satin. Two piece sleeves have gold damask undersleeves and sheer embroidered oversleeves. Embroidery also covers bodice front. Exceptional.* **Value: $800.00**

Plate 50: *Velvet coat, ca. 1892-94. Fur-trimmed toggles. Leg of mutton sleeves.* **Value: $425.00**

1895

Chapter IV
The Gibson Girl 1900-1909

Plate 51: The Gibson Girl Silhouette. *Pouched pigeon breast front and small waist. This satin day dress has pagoda sleeves and a lace collar and yoke. Ca. 1905.*

Common Characteristics

Emphasis on fine detail, such as tucking, lace inserts, delicate embroidery.
Blouse style bodice, pouched in front or all around.
Skirt fitted to the hips, flares out at bottom.
Boning at every seam in lining of bodice, lining fastens separately, before 1904.
No boning after 1903, tapes that tie around waist at center back of bodice.

General Information

By 1899, economic recovery was in full swing, businesses boomed, fortunes were made, and lost, overnight. After a decade of scrimping, money was available and freely spent. Fashion luxuriated in expensive silks, chiffons and laces which were literally allowed to trail on the ground over muddy paths and dusty streets. Maneuvering these long, trailing skirts was difficult without exposing a glimpse of the beautiful and equally expensive embroidered, lace and ribboned petticoat worn beneath. The economic boom was short-lived however, and by 1907 recessionary trends were beginning to be felt in the fashion industry.

The silhouette called the "S-Curve" or "Gibson Bend" dominated this period. It was characterized by the bodice being pouched forward in a style that is sometimes called the "pigeon breast" or "kangaroo pouch," the tightly corsetted waistline pushing the hips slightly back, the skirt flowing down to the ground. Charles Dana Gibson immortalized this style with his famous "Gibson Girls" drawings.

The two piece dress with a separate bodice and skirt was typical until 1903. After 1904, one piece dresses were also seen, skirt and bodice being attached at the waistband.

Emphasis throughout this period was on soft, full, feminine dresses made of the most luxurious fabrics. The softest of silks, transparent crepe de chines, flimsy chiffons, and cotton batistes abounded. Lace was the most popular form of trimming, and dresses made entirely of lace were seen.

White was the most popular color, often worn unbroken by any other color and many dresses of this period are mistaken for bridal gowns.

The Bodice

A major change in bodice construction occurred in this period. With the introduction of the shirtwaist style, the forerunner to modern "blouses," around 1900, bodices appeared more blouse-like. The first shirtwaists were only loose in appearance, that is, they were mounted on a fully-boned lining which fit tightly, the lining fastening separately with hooks and eyes center front. The pouched portion of the outer fabric fastened generally at the shoulder and under the arm. In 1903, some shirtwaists fastened center back. A waistband of softly folded fabric was attached to the shirtwaist and fastened separately at the side, back or front. All shirtwaists were worn drooping over the waistband of the skirt in front, backs still being tightly fitted in the fashion of earlier bodices (see Plates 52 and 60). Skirts and shirtwaists still hooked together center back until 1904.

In 1904, boning was eliminated from the shirtwaist, although a bone at each side seam might still be found in some dresses until around 1910. The unboned shirtwaists had tapes or ties at the center back of the waist that tied together around the waist (see Plate 55). These shirtwaists were worn tucked inside the waistband of the skirt so the tapes were not visible. These loose, shapeless shirtwaists pouched not only in the front but in back as well and were generally not lined. The back of the shirtwaist was usually cut somewhat shorter than the front.

Jacket bodices were seen again, fastening center front with or without lapels, and were most popular at the end of the period. (See Plate 64.)

After 1904, with the exception of jacket bodices, most shirtwaists fastened center back with hooks and eyes or small pearl buttons. Decorative buttons were also found, with actual hooks and eyes fastening underneath. Very large, fancy buttons were popular after 1906.

Collars were still worn very high and some, when made of a flimsy material, were held up by bones. Most high collars still fastened separately center back until 1904. An occasionally seen alternative was a plain, round neckline encircling the base of the throat, appearing around 1905, foreshadowing a new trend. These appeared first in informal housedresses or for travelling dress (see Plate 54). The "peter pan" collar appeared around 1908 (see Plates 56 and 64) and by 1909 the lower neckline was acceptable in all forms of day wear. (See Plate 59.)

Sleeves in 1900 were still fairly fitted and became fuller as the period progressed. Bishop style sleeves were most popular and after 1901, sleeves often had an extra pouch of fullness between the elbow and wrist. Tiered or pagoda sleeves were seen beginning in 1902 (see Plates 51 and 53). Sleeves were worn generally long and ended in a cuff or point over the back of the hand until 1902 when very full, puffy, elbow length sleeves appeared for day wear (see Plate 61). Unlike the 1890s full sleeves, these were unlined. Lace sleeves with ribboned cuffs were also popular. (See Plate 58.)

After 1907, shirtwaist trimmings tended to run vertically and shoulder pleating became very popular. Sleeves were often set-in under a pleat of fabric at the shoulder (see Plates 59 and 63). Contrasting yokes were popular, usually the yoke and collar being of the same fabric and fastening separately in back while the shirtwaist itself fastened center front or to the side (see Plate 63). These details are among the confusing styles that look very much like the 1890s; however, construction techniques had changed so dramatically in 15 years with the elimination of boning and lining, and with the shirtwaist now tucking into the waistband of the skirt or in one piece construction, they should not confuse the knowledgeable collector.

Plate 52: *Brown and white silk day dress trimmed with lace. Trained skirt, pagoda sleeves. Ca. 1903.* **Value: $325.00**

Plate 53: *Close-up, pagoda sleeve.*

Plate 54: *Glazed cotton travelling dress. Note lower neckline. Three pieces with matching purse. Belt is boned. Ca. 1906.* **Value as is with minor alterations: $175.00**

Plate 55: *Back view from inside. Typical bodice construction after 1904. Note ties at waistband.*

Plate 56: *Glazed cotton and wool day dress. Eyelet peter pan collar and trim. Survives with matching cape. Suitable for half mourning. Ca. 1909.* **Value as a set: $295.00**

Plate 57: *Matching wool cape with lace applique trim.*

Plate 58: *Day dress of embroidered limerick lace trimmed with duchesse lace and applique lace, cuffs trimmed with silk ribbon. Ca. 1909.* **Value: $495.00**

Plate 59: *Close-up, front view. Note lower neckline common beginning in 1909.*

Plate 60: *Black and white wool day dress trimmed with satin. Trained skirt. Ca. 1901.* Value: $250.00

Plate 61: *White batiste cotton wedding gown with lace inserts and tiered skirt. Ca. 1905.* Value: $495.00

The Skirt

The gored skirt was still worn at the beginning of the period, but with a difference. Beginning in 1899, a horizontal band of trimming was often found located at knee level from which the skirt flared out into a slight train measuring up to 6½ yards around the hem (see Plate 52). These skirts were generally not lined to preserve their fluidness. They were meant to be worn covering the feet in front as well as flaring out into a train at back. Until 1903, trimming was limited to flat bands (see Plate 60). Skirts made entirely of sheer lace or lace netting were also seen, these meant to be worn with a colored petticoat (see Plate 109). Center back fastening was no longer the rule and some skirts fastened on the side.

After 1903, skirts became fuller and for everyday wear were no longer worn trained. Some skirts had belts in coordinating fabrics and belts made of soft fabrics were sometimes boned (see Plate 62). Deep boned waistbands were seen in some skirts beginning in 1906, these skirts known as "corselet skirts." Beginning in 1904, skirts were often very decorated (see Plate 54) and briefly, in 1905 and 1906, skirts with two or three tiers of flounces were seen. (See Plate 61.)

The decorated skirt quickly fell out of fashion, however, and by 1907 skirts fell unhampered by excess trimmings (see Plate 63). Skirts with kick pleats were popular at the end of the period.

In 1908, the first narrow skirts were introduced in Paris (see Plate 68). These, however, did not catch on in general popularity until around 1910.

Evening Dress

Evening dress resembled day dress in all manner except for its low neckline. The evening neckline of this period that was cut very low and wide, with shoulder straps, was most common for this period. These were often finished with a row or two of deep flounces of lace or tulle. Shoulders were nearly always exposed.

Outerwear

Capes continued to be popular, the high standing collar disappearing midway through this period (see Plate 57). These were not so excessively decorated as in previous periods. Long coats became popular, with full sleeves gathered in a band at the wrist. These often had large, flat collars either square or rounded which fastened at the throat. Fur became a popular material for outer wear, either as trim or as the main material of the piece. Fur stoles were the most popular often with the heads of the creatures still attached. Fur muffs and jackets were also seen, the most worn being sables and ermine. Most outerwear of this period was plainly trimmed compared to those in earlier decades.

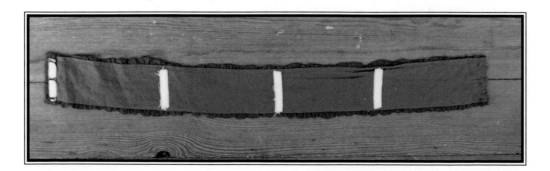

Plate 62: *Close-up, boned belt.*

Plate 63: *Watered silk day dress with satin yoke and cuffs. Buttons on left side with fancy steel cut buttons. Ca. 1907.* **Value: $250.00**

Plate 64: *Jacket-style day dress, yellow wool with blue stripes. Buttons center front. Peter pan collar. Ca. 1908.* **Value: $135.00**

Undergarments

Petticoats, camisoles and chemise slips of this period are highly collectible because they were as beautiful during this period as many dresses.

The skirt, which flared out at the knees, required a petticoat underneath to help it stand out. Also, the very long skirts with trains of the early years necessitated the use of beautiful laces and trimmings since the petticoat would be seen when the skirt was lifted to climb a stair or enter a carriage, These petticoats were normally made of white cotton or linen and had deep flounces of lace at their hems. (See Plates 65 and 66.)

Camisoles pouched in front and all around to support the pouched Gibson Girl bodices. The very transparent fabrics so much in vogue necessitated that camisoles also be well-made and beautiful. (See Plate 65.)

The combination, which is sometimes called by other names such as "the Lenora" or "chemise slip," was a one piece garment which was, in effect, a camisole attached to pantaloons with an overskirt. These were generally made of a fine white muslin or linen and trimmed with lace. (See Plate 67.)

Price Valuations:

The most valuable of this period are the beautifully detailed white shirtwaists and dresses which are popular among brides today.

White shirtwaists or blouses in transparent cotton batiste (with lace inserts or embroidered, very fine details)	$85.00 – 300.00
White dresses, cotton batiste, lace, chiffon with elaborate trim	$300.00 – 800.00
Other colors, everyday dresses	$85.00 – 250.00
Other colors, special occasion dresses	$250.00 – 400.00
Capes and coats, little trim	$50.00 – 95.00
Fur stoles and wraps	$45.00 – 200.00
Lace-trimmed petticoats	$125.00 – 200.00
Camisoles	$40.00 – 65.00
Combinations	$125.00 – 175.00

Plate 65: *Camisole and petticoat, white linen with crochet lace trim. Ca. 1900.*
Value: camisole, $58.00; petticoat, $145.00

Plate 66: *Linen petticoat with deep lace, double flounce hem. Ca. 1900.* **Value:** $195.00

Plate 67: *Combination with drawstring neckline, petite lace trim. Ca. 1905.* **Value:** $125.00

Plate 68: *Cotton batiste day dress with crochet lace trim. One piece construction. Pearl buttons. Ca. 1908.* **Value: $325.00**

Plate 69: *Close up of crochet lace trim.*

Plate 70: *Cotton batiste shirtwaist, lace inserts in front and on sleeves, hand embroidered front, lace cuffs. Ca. 1909.* **Value: $275.00**

Plate 71: *Cotton batiste shirtwaist, lace inserts in front, lace collar. Ca. 1907.* **Value: $175.00**

1902

Chapter V
The Tailored Years 1910-1918

Plate 72: The Tailored Silhouette. *Practical clothing with slim lines. Trimming is kept to the minimum. This woman wears a jacket-style tunic with a tiered skirt. Ca. 1913.*

"The length of sleeves begins at the wrist and ends at the shoulders. You can wear them where you like, but not when you like. For example, the long sleeve belongs to the morning, the elbow or three-quarter length sleeve to the afternoon, but the dress that is practically sleeveless or where the sleeve exists but does not reach the elbow is used only for evening purposes.

Everything is narrow — shoulders, back, hips and dresses. A few short skirts are two yards wide at the base. Two yards and a quarter and two yards and a half are conservative widths. You can go as far and as fast as you like in any of them with perfect comfort. It is only the extreme widths that look ridiculous. The others are pretty if you like to look slender."

The Delineator
March 1911

"First of all, to repeat what every woman knows, the narrow skirt is as past as last year's weather."

Needlecraft
April 1915

Common Characteristics

Simplified dresses, both in trimming and construction technique.
Snaps seen beginning around 1915.
One piece dresses fasten center back.
Bodices fasten at the front, often to one side of the neckline.

General Information

The period between 1910 and 1918 was marked by economic recession and the trauma of World War I. The war's effect on fashion was almost immediate. Dresses at the beginning of the war were extremely feminine, bedecked with frills and lace, trimmed with an air of optimism, patriotism and gaiety. As the war lingered, much graver than anticipated, women's fashions eschewed frills and adopted a more uniform, practical style. Many military influences were seen on dresses of this period, such as sailor collars and military style buttons. By the end of the war, women's clothing had been reduced to the bare minimum necessitated by war rationing and the new roles women took on for the war effort.

Throughout this period, there was a general trend toward simplification in dress, in trimmings and construction techniques. Dresses fell into four basic categories:

1. The one piece dress often called a "frock." (See Plate 83.)
2. The separate blouse and skirt, with blouse tucking into a high-waisted, deep-boned waistband of a corselet skirt. (See Plate 73.)
3. The separate "tunic" and skirt, the tunic flaring out bell-shaped over a narrow skirt. (See Plate 72.)
4. The separate jacket and skirt. (See Plate 78.)

The fashionable silhouette for most of the period was slender, narrow and tubelike with a high waistline. To achieve the higher waistline, dress construction had to change and many dresses beginning in 1910 were made up in one piece. These dresses generally fastened center back with hooks and eyes, though buttons (often only decorative) were also seen, as well as buttons and hooks used alternately.

Transparent fabrics such as voile and very fine muslin were most popular with soft woolens and serges used for winter wear. Trimmings were generally subdued, eyelet was popular as well as many forms of embroidery. Soft pleats, delicate edging and large buttons were common. Lace jabots and under-cuffs were also seen.

White remained a popular color in the beginning of this period along with shades of yellow, tan and sand. There was a tendency in one piece dresses to make the bodice a contrasting color from the skirt. Colors became generally bolder and brighter as the period progressed.

Plate 73: *Two piece voile pneumonia blouse and matching skirt. Sailor collar with lace trim, high-waisted corselet skirt. Ca. 1913.* **Value: $275.00**

Plate 74: *Detail, lace trimming in front. Buttons on left side with pearl buttons.*

The Bodice

The shirtwaist of the previous period was still worn, with a round neckline or peter pan collar; some retained a high standing collar until about 1912. Sailor-style collars were introduced in 1911 and were first worn in a contrasting color from the blouse. These collars normally circled around the back of the neck and buttoned on the side of the neckline (see Plate 73). The square neckline was the most fashionable after 1912, often edged with flats bands of lace (see Plate 74). V-shaped necklines and crossover fronts with a "modesty" insert center front were also seen (see Plate 81). A high standing collar at the back, but open in a V or square at the front, was introduced after 1915.

Lingerie blouses, simply cut from fine voile or other transparent materials, became popular around 1910. These were worn with a slight V or rounded neckline at first, later with the common square neckline. Delicate embroidery often in conjunction with beading in intricate patterns decorated these fragile blouses. The introduction of the lingerie blouse with a low square neckline bordered by narrow reveres (square or rectangular shaped lapels) for day time wear caused a sensation around 1913 (see Plate 73). It was the first time in over 70 years that such a daringly low neckline appeared in day wear and the shocking fashion was severely condemned by the pulpit. Physicians also took a stand with warnings that wearing such blouses would increase women's risk of upper respiratory disease. A contemporary journalist dubbed the fashion "the pneumonia blouse," and its popularity soared. By 1914, the square neckline was incorporated into all forms of day wear.

Sleeves, which were still fairly full in 1909, became more fitted around 1910. Kimono sleeves, cut in one piece with the bodice, were popular until about 1917 (see Plate 75). After 1915, fitted, full-length sleeves ending in a cuff as well as ¾-length sleeves were most often seen.

Jacket bodices were worn fastening center front in three very different styles: a high-waisted jacket with coat tails worn over a vest and blouse known as a "Directoire Suit;" a boxy jacket worn closed (see Plate 77); and the tailored suit worn open with a blouse. (See Plate 78.)

By 1917, blouses were no longer worn tucked into the high waistline, but over the skirt ending at hip level, held to the waist by a sash or belt, setting the silhouette for the 1920s.

Plate 75: *Lingerie blouse with kimono sleeves, blue hand embroidery. Ca. 1910.* **Value: $85.00**

Plate 76: *Batiste cotton day dress with crochet lace trim, elastic waistband, fastens in front on left with snaps. Double tiered skirt. Sailor collar. Meant to be worn 7 inches off ground. Ca. 1917.* **Value: $145.00**

Plate 77: *Wool jacket and skirt with large pockets. Ca. 1918.* **Value: $65.00**

Plate 78: *Tailor-made, jacket bodice and skirt. Ca. 1910.* **Value: $95.00**

The Skirt

By 1911, the narrow, tubular skirt became the most common with little trimming, mostly large, nonfunctional buttons. The waistline by 1912 was very high, just under the bustline. Skirts that were separate from the blouse had deep waistbands which were boned and were known as corselet skirts (see Plate 86). Many skirts that were attached to the bodice also had bones at the waistband. From 1912-1914, skirts became so narrow that walking was inhibited — thus being dubbed "hobble skirts." Side seams of these skirts were usually slashed open, a piece of lace or contrasting fabric sewn inside, although some daring women revealed their legs this way.

An overskirt ending at knee level was sometimes seen before 1912 and by 1914 overskirts with one or more tiers in varying degrees of fullness were seen (see Plates 76 and 79). These overskirts were attached either to the skirt itself or to the bodice, and this tunic might form the first in a series of tiers (see Plate 72). Beginning in 1914, skirts with a slight inverted V-opening at the hem in front were seen.

By 1915, the impractical, narrow skirts with their ankle-revealing slits were replaced with shorter, fuller, more comfortable skirts which were worn 7 to 8 inches off the ground. These shorter skirts foreshadowed trends to follow in the 1920s. These skirts were circular or bell-shaped; some gathered around in an elastic band (see Plate 76) and others were sewn onto a fitted hip yoke. Briefly, skirts measuring as much as 5 yards around the hem were seen in 1915, although most skirts of this period measured between 2½ and 3 yards.

Waistlines were worn roughly 2 inches above the natural waist level in 1915 and dropped to natural level by 1919.

Evening Dress

With the introduction of the low neckline in day wear, evening wear was no longer differentiated by the neckline. Instead, sleeve length became an important factor, the sleeves being above elbow length for evenings. Trains were also worn for evening, the narrow fishtail train appearing around 1912 (see Plate 82). Very formal ball gowns still dipped low on the shoulders.

Lampshade skirts, a bell-shaped overskirt with asymmetrical hemlines worn over a narrow underskirt, were seen on evening dresses between 1912 and 1914. (See Plate 79.)

Silks and satins were most popular for evening wear. Beading was a favored trim for evening dresses of this period and ostrich feathers were also seen.

Outerwear

Coats of this period were long and loose with little or no trimming (see Plate 84). The sack-style coat, trench coat and raglan coat all echoed military styles. Fur stoles were still popular, with heads and tails attached.

Price Valuations

Lingerie and pneumonia blouses with delicate trims	$65.00 – 95.00
Everyday dresses, little trim	$65.00 – 200.00
White cotton batiste, eyelet and lace dresses	$145.00 – 350.00
Special occasion dresses, elaborate trim	$250.00 – 400.00
Coats	$75.00 – 200.00
Fur stoles	$45.00 – 95.00

Plate 79: *Black taffeta evening gown, ostrich feathers trim neckline and overskirt hem. Velvet trim and cloth roses encircle back side of bodice. Lampshade-style skirt of taffeta with slim underskirt of silk and netting. Ca. 1912.* **Value:** *$285.00*

Plate 80: *Back view.*

Plate 81: *Coral silk evening gown, trimmed with sequins, beads and rhinestones. Fishtail train. Ca. 1914.* **Value:** *$330.00*

Plate 82: *Back view.*

Plate 83: *Embroidered eyelet day dress, one piece, back fastening with hooks and eyes. Ca. 1910.* **Value: $300.00**

Plate 84: *Sack style dust coat. Ca. 1915.* **Value: $95.00**

Plate 85: *Green linen day dress with lace yoke. One piece, back fastening with hooks and eyes. Ca. 1911.* **Value: $125.00**

Plate 86: *Inside detail, boned corselet waistband. Ca. 1913.*

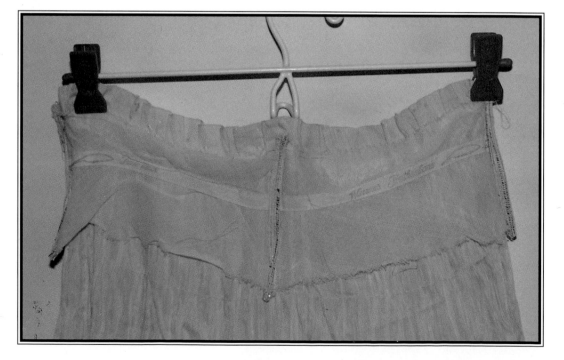

1912

The Chemise Dress

Bodices and skirts now melded into the one piece chemise dress without a waistline or with the waistline at the hips. The chemise was constructed simply, seamed together at the shoulders with two side seams with or without two piece sleeves. All added trim was then applied to this basic form.

The first chemise dresses appeared around 1919. These early dresses might or might not have had waistlines. The waistline, if apparent, was a little below the natural level (see Plate 88). They normally fastened with snaps on the left side underneath the arm hole. The skirt narrowed at the hem and some skirts had elastic threaded through the hem to hold it in. By 1921, the waistline was around the hips and most dresses simply slipped on over the head without fasteners of any type.

Many dresses of the early 1920s showed an Oriental influence and were trimmed with Chinese-type motifs and tassels. The discovery of King Tut's tomb in 1923 brought an Egyptian influence into trimmings and also a tendency toward darker "Egyptian" colors such as red and dark blue.

In 1920, Coco Chanel introduced the hemline that was worn 9 inches off the ground, however most hemlines of the first years were still worn 7 – 8 inches off the ground. In 1924, hemlines reached the knee level and in 1925 knees were exposed for the first time. At the same time, sleeves disappeared completely in most day dress, except for winter wear which might have long, tight sleeves to the wrist. Matching jackets began to appear with some sleeveless dresses at this time and would remain fashionable into the next decade. These jackets generally did not have collars and were sometimes trimmed with braid. Around 1927, uneven hemlines were seen (see Plate 89) and by 1928, scarf-like panels of flimsy material fell around the hems of many skirts. Skinny belts made of matching fabric and tied around the hip were also popular at this time (see Plate 90). Skirt hems dropped below the knee around 1929, coinciding with the stock market crash and were worn approximately 14 inches off the ground.

Late in the period, designers began to cut fabric on the cross-grain so that it clung to the figure, once more outlining curves, foreshadowing fashions of the next decade.

Plate 88: *Organdy chemise dress with waistline a little below the waist. Ca. 1919.* **Value: $45.00**

Plate 89: *Crepe chemise dress with asymmetrical hem. Lace yoke. Ca. 1927.* **Value: $65.00**

Plate 90: *Cotton print chemise dress with lace yoke and cuffs. Fabric belt ties around hips. Originally worn as a wedding gown. Ca. 1929.* **Value: $55.00**

Blouses

The lingerie blouse continued to be worn in a form more boxy and unadorned than previously seen (see Plate 91). It generally fastened at the shoulder or to one side of the front neckline with snaps.

Evening Dress

Evening dress varied little from day dress, the same chemise style was seen but necklines plunged lower (see Plate 92). "Court trains" were introduced in formal evening dress. These are knee length at the front hem but had a panel-like train falling onto the floor in the back. Evening dresses were generally more trimmed, with beading being most popular; however rows of lace and tasseled fringes were also seen.

Outerwear

The main form of outerwear continued to be the coat. Fur coats came into fashion primarily made of fox, squirrel, raccoon or moleskin and fur trimmings were seen on the collars and cuffs of cloth coats. Briefly, in 1922, monkey fur was popular. Coats followed the general barrel silhouette, were boxy and loose-fitting, and most wrapped around the wearer and fastened at the side. Turned-over lapels which ended at hip level or below were popular.

Price Valuations

Elaborately beaded dresses are most valued among collectors.

Lingerie blouses	$45.00 – 125.00
Everyday chemise dresses, little trim	$40.00 – 75.00
Special occasion chemise dresses, elaborate trim	$125.00 – 800.00
Fur coats	$200.00 – 400.00

Plate 91: *Hand-beaded lingerie blouse. Ca. 1919.* **Value: $95.00**

Plate 92: *Silk evening chemise dress with rhinestones in front, beaded fringe, rhinestone belt buckle. Ca. 1926.* **Value: $485.00**

Plate 93: *Cotton chemise with flounced yoke. Ca. 1924.* **Value: $40.00**

Plate 94: *Black silk and brocaded silk chemise dress with belt. Ca. 1921.* **Value: $50.00**

Chapter VII
The Depression Era 1930-1940

Plate 95: The Depression Years. *Simple, clinging dresses once again emphasizing the Hour Glass Silhouette. Young woman graduate, ca. 1934.*

> *"Skirt lengths bring a surprise this season. For daytime they are two or three inches longer than they were last summer. This brings them fairly well over the calf of the leg. Formal afternoon gowns remain ankle length."*
>
> **Ladies' Home Journal**
> **November 1930**

Common Characteristics

One piece dresses, reaching mid-calf length.
Fabric is cut on the bias.
Dress slips over the head without fasteners; or snaps, or zips up the side under the arm.

General Information

Unemployment, poverty, soup kitchens, the repeal of prohibition, and the first government welfare programs. This was the Depression Era. The fun of the 1920s was over. Women's skirts plunged from the above knee flapper dress to the more conservative mid-calf length. Depression era fashions reflected the economy with their practical, washable fabrics, little or no trimmings. Even among the wealthy, it became bad taste to flaunt one's wealth. The most elegant evening gowns were plainly trimmed and evening dresses made of cotton were sometimes seen.

Fashion designers, suffering from decreased sales and the onslaught of ready-wear clothing made possible by the simple styles of the 1920s, attempted to revive their industry by introducing floor length gowns for evening and formal wear.

Plate 96: *Purple velvet dress with puffed sleeves. Typical diamond pattern center front. Ca. 1935.* **Value: $235.00**

Plate 97: *Close-up of typical 1930s puffed sleeves.*

Day Dress

The most common day dress of the 1930s was still the one piece dress. These were normally cut on the bias, that is, diagonally against the weave of the fabric, so that the material clings more readily to the wearer. Gone was the barrel silhouette. The new silhouette was softer, more feminine and accentuated, once again, the hour glass figure.

The waistline was back to normal level in 1928. By 1930, it dipped in the back, but stayed at normal level in the front. Many dresses of the mid-1930s do not have a waistline per se, but the entire waist area was cut from a diamond or triangle-shaped piece of fabric, the top point beginning at the bustline (see Plate 96). Side panels were narrow and fitted through the hips then widening, so that the skirt flared out around mid-thigh level (see Plate 102). This cut was seen on most one piece dresses between 1931 and 1936. Most dresses of the 1930s slipped over the head without fasteners or fastened with snaps on the side under the arm.

Zippers appeared. They were first introduced in expensive sportswear in the 1920s. Coco Chanel began using them on dresses in 1931. By 1935, they were found on more moderate priced fashions, replacing snaps under the arm as the most common fastener. Late in the period, fabric-covered buttons appeared fastening down the back of some more formal dresses.

In 1936, a narrower skirt was seen (see Plate 101) with a tighter waistline often accentuated with a belt made of the same fabric as the dress or a stiff peplum at the back. Many dresses had ties sewn at the waistline which tied together at the back. "Pin" pleats, very narrow pleats often of crinkled crepe, were popular on skirts.

The caped shoulder (see Plates 95 and 98) appeared around 1930. These were often sleeveless. The fitted sleeve was the most common sleeve until around 1935-36 when short puffed sleeves appeared. These were generally gathered in one or two lines of stitching throughout the length of the sleeve (see Plate 97). Beginning in 1936, these often had small shoulder pads added under them, foreshadowing the large, padded shoulders of the 1940s. (See Plate 100.)

Necklines in the early 1930s were most often rounded at the base of the throat, V-shaped or scoop necked. Heart-shaped necklines were seen beginning around 1935.

Many new synthetic fabrics were introduced in the 1930s, including the "elasticized" fabrics which made it possible to slip on a clingy dress without the use of fasteners. Popular fabrics in the 1930s were rayon, velvet, synthetic crepes, and cottons for everyday wear.

Plate 98: *Backless evening gown in cut velvet, cape sleeves. Ca. 1931.* **Value: $295.00**

Plate 99: *Back view.*

Plate 100: *Blue velvet and rayon dress with V-neckline, puffed sleeves with small shoulder pads. Ca. 1936.* **Value: $190.00**

Plate 101: *Satin gown with lace trim. Originally worn as a wedding dress, cut short and dyed blue by original owner. Ca. 1938.* **Value: $85.00**

Evening Dress

Evening dress varied from day dress by the length of the skirt, floor length for the most formal occasions. A puffed sleeve which ended at the elbow appeared in formal evening wear in 1930. Many evening dresses were backless with a flowing cape from the shoulders (see Plate 99). Satin and velvet were the most popular fabrics for evening gowns. Trimmings were subdued, cloth flowers and beads being the most popular.

Outerwear

Fur was the word for outerwear of the 1930s. Synthetic furs, such as mohair, were popular in long coats (see Plate 103). Sweaters and jackets with large fur collars that bordered a deep V-shaped neckline abounded (see Plate 104). Popular furs were soft: Persian lamb, black seal and, in the later 1930s, mink.

Plate 102: *Wedding gown of satin trimmed with satin flowers with pearl-tipped stamens. Cloche veil with wax flowers and pearl beads and cathedral length train trimmed with lace. Ca. 1932.* **Value as a set: $495.00**

Price Valuations

Velvet dresses and floor length gowns currently bring the highest prices.

Everyday dresses, little trim	$35.00 – 75.00
Special occasion dresses	$75.00 – 400.00
Fur coats	$75.00 – 200.00
Fur collared jackets and sweaters	$30.00 – 75.00

Plate 103: *Mohair coat with mink tail clasp. Ca. 1938.* **Value: $100.00**

Plate 104: *Sweater with mink collar. Ca. 1936.* **Value: $45.00**

Plate 105: *Chemise dress in navy blue with lace yoke and jabot. Ca. 1930.* **Value: $35.00**

Plate 106: *Rayon dress with velvet trim, cloth flower at base of neckline. Originally worn as a wedding dress. Ca. 1936.* **Value: $45.00**

1932

Chapter VIII
Dress For Weddings, Funerals and Sports

Plate 107: Wedding couple. *Bride wears tubular dress of light color trimmed with dark lace. Ca. 1879.*

Wedding Dress

The white wedding gown was first popularized by Queen Victoria who wore white on her wedding day. In the 1840s and 1850s, many brides followed suit. However, the nineteenth century and early twentieth century bride had her choice of colors and usually chose a color which was fashionable that particular season and could be worn again as a "best dress."

The most colorful bridal gowns were seen in the 1870s and 1880s when wine colors, browns and even blue-blacks were fashionable (see Plate 107). Softly tinted pastels were a popular bridal gown choice in the 1890s when the brides-maids were dressed in white gowns. White was the most popular choice for brides shortly after 1900 when white was popular for all forms of summer wear (see Plate 61). By 1910, colors were back in fashion and in the 1920s bridal gowns were often just as colorful and short in skirt length as normal day wear (see Plate 90). There was an attempt by fashion designers to bring hemlines back to the floor in the late 1920s. This resulted in some 1920s wedding dresses having a short, knee-exposing front hem but a long "court train" at the back. Formal gowns of the 1930s were floor length, and so many formal wedding gowns were also worn floor length. It became fashionable again, in the 1930s, to wear white for bridal gowns, and hence the long, white "traditional" wedding gown was born (see Plate 102). During these practical Depression Era years, many was the bride who cut her wedding gown short and dyed it a different color so she might wear it again as a "best dress" (see Plate 101). Still, in the 1930s, it was not uncommon for a bride to be married in a short, colorful dress. (See Plate 106.)

Bridesmaids generally wore dresses of their own choice, consulting with the bride and other bridesmaids to be sure colors would not clash and that they would not, of course, "outshine" the bride.

Styles for wedding dress followed the fashionable styles of either day dress or evening dress, depending on the hour of the day the wedding was performed. If the newlyweds were to commence on their honeymoon shortly after the cere-mony, the bride often wore a travelling dress. These were comfortable dresses in dark, washable fabrics and often had a slightly lower neckline than normal day dress. In the 1890s and early 1900s, the neckline of the travelling dress was around the base of the throat. (See Plate 54.)

The bridal veil was often the only thing distinguishing the bride from others at the wedding. Her veil was invari-ably white lace or white lace netting (see Plate 108). Favorite trimmings in the nineteenth century were orange blos-soms and rosebuds, either of cloth or real flowers. Long cathedral length veils with "cloche" type head pieces were common in the 1920s and 1930s. (See Plate 102.)

Plate 108: *Bridal veil, 1890s. Duchesse lace headpiece is trimmed with cloth flowers and beads. Satin ribbons stand up at front and trail down the back of the veil. Veil is made of applique lace.* **Value: $75.00**

> *"Violet has not been worn in second mourning for a long time till this season. It has only lately made its appearance."*
>
> Demorest's Monthly Magazine
> December 1880

Mourning Dress

Dresses for funerals and proper periods of mourning were very much governed by the rules of etiquette in the nineteenth and early twentieth centuries. The proper periods were as follows:

death of husband	30 months
death of parent	24 months
death of grandparent	9 months
death of child	9 months
death of sibling	6 months
death of aunt/uncle	3 months
death of wife	3 months

"Deep mourning" was the first twelve months after the death of a husband. Victorian widows in deep mourning wore black crepe dresses without trimmings. Plain black crepe veils were worn over the head. The veils were worn longer with wider hems at the beginning of the deep mourning period. Black crepe, in its finest form, had the tendency to turn brown after much wear and shredded easily. This tattered, brown appearance is where the term "widow's weeds" came from. Crepe was seen less after 1900 when deep mourning dresses were of black silk or serge, sometimes trimmed with crinkled, crepe-like material.

After 12 months of deep mourning, the widow discarded crepe as a fabric and dresses of other fabrics could be worn. These were still black, unbroken by any color. Still the widow could not wear jewels or any trimming considered too frivolous. After 18 months, the widow entered "half mourning" and could wear black dresses trimmed with black ribbons or black lace (see Plate 109) as well as white collars and white cuffs (see Plate 56). Other suitable trimmings at this time included black embroidery, bands of black velvet, jet and black glass beads, black jewelry and buttons, but these would have a dull or half-dull finish. Not until the full mourning period was over could the widow wear any other clothes.

It was suitable for a widow to go out socially after 12 months of mourning, and black tulle and crepe-trimmed evening dresses were sometimes found. Evening dresses as well as hats and bonnets for daytime wear were trimmed with "mourning flowers," these being white roses, jasmine or violets without foliage or with black velvet or black silk leaves.

Beginning in 1880, black, silver, gray and violet were the suitable colors for "second mourning" of more distant relatives, friends, or in some instances, a high ranking government official.

Plate 109: *Appropriate wear for a widow in half mourning. Black netting trimmed with black lace and ribbons. Ca. 1900.* **Value: $300.00**

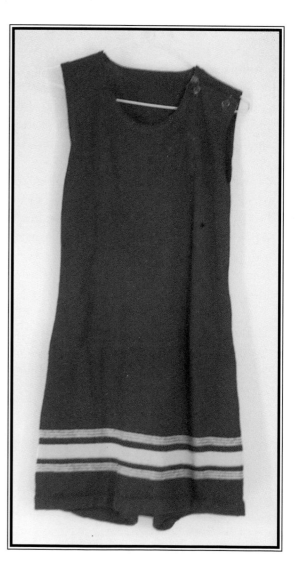

Plate 110: *Unisex wool bathing suit. Ca. 1924.* **Value: $65.00**

"Yesterday, I hired a gentleman's or ladies' — it was bisexual — bathing dress and swam far out, until the seagulls played over my head, mistaking me for a drifting sea anemone."

Virginia Woolfe
1909

Sportswear

The nineteenth century brought about several innovations in sportswear for women. The bathing suit which appeared first in the 1860s had loose-fitting, elbow length sleeves and bloomer-like leggings reaching well below the knee. By around 1905, slimmer, heavy wool one piece suits were worn. The early suits had legs that reached to knee level or just below and short sleeves. By 1920, the sleeveless model which buttoned at the shoulder with short legs covered by a short skirt appeared (see Plate 110). The same styles were often worn by both men and women into the 1930s.

Wool bloomers became fashionable first for bicycling in the 1890s and were worn by other women athletes well into the next century. These can be dated by their bodice styles which echo that of fashionable day dress. (See Plate 111.)

The bloomers of the 1920s were less full and cut more like men's trousers. They were worn with tailored shirts and ties that resembled men's neckties. (See Plate 112.)

Two innovations of the 1920s in sportswear were long pants for women, introduced first for snow skiing, and the zipper. The zipper appeared on very expensive ski wear, sports jackets and tennis costumes where it tested the water before being introduced in general day wear in the 1930s.

Price Valuations

Wedding/Mourning Dresses same as special occasion dresses of the period (see previous chapters).

Wedding Veils	$75.00 – 125.00
Swimming Suits	$25.00 – 125.00
Bloomer Costumes, 1890-1920	$125.00 – 225.00
Sportswear, 1920-1940	$45.00 – 85.00

Plate 111: *Young women's ball team in bloomers. Ca. 1910.*

Plate 112: *Woman in bloomers. Ca. 1929.*

Chapter IX
Hats and Bonnets

Plate 113: *Woman in one of the larger hats, around 1897.*

The importance of millinery is sometimes hard for our bareheaded generation to grasp. It was, however, in the nineteenth and early twentieth centuries the milliner's bill that was cited as the second most expensive household account. No costume was complete without an exquisite and matching hat or bonnet, and in times when economics or politics dictated stern and practical fashions, the hat remained the last epitome of frivolity, the essence of femininity, and the glory of conspicuous consumption.

Unfortunately for collectors, few hats remain unchanged or undamaged by time. Many hats were remade into the newest styles as fashions changed, many more fell to destruction in the toy boxes of children. Those that survive often do so minus some of their trimmings, especially whole birds, wings, etc., which do not tolerate the heat and dust of attic trunks. Trimmings, especially expensive feathers, were often scavenged for new hats or other costumes. It is, in fact, a miracle that so many hats do survive and these should be cherished as precious reminders of more gracious days.

Though individual hats vary incredibly, each milliner being an artist of her/his time, basic shapes and styles can be traced through the years.

The most common form of head wear in the 1850s was the bonnet with strings that tied under the chin. Bonnets of this period framed the face in an oval and often the inside of the brim was trimmed with flowers (see Plate 115). This style remained in fashion into the 1860s, however, earlier bonnets generally had a "curtain" at the back, that is a piece of material covering the back of the neck, but after 1863 the curtain was no longer seen. The general shape of the bonnet changed in 1860 to more spoon-shaped, the crown rising higher on the head. These spoon bonnets were worn throughout the 1860s. (See Plate 114.)

Bonnets of the 1850s and 1860s were invariably made of a wire foundation onto which the material was sewn. Transparent materials such as net were used for formal bonnets, and velvets and silks were also seen. They were trimmed with feathers, ribbons, and flowers.

In the 1860s, the hat began to gain popularity. A small round hat, called a pork pie hat, appeared first in 1860. This looked very much like the 1950s pill box style. It was worn tilted far forward on the forehead, was usually trimmed with a tuft of small feathers at one side and was fashionable with young women.

The small sailor-style hat appeared in 1863 with a round crown and a narrow brim. These hats were usually made of straw and trimmed with ribbon. The sailor hat continued in popularity until the end of the century and gradually grew larger. (See Plate 121.)

Plate 114: *Spoon bonnet of netting, dyed ostrich feather trim. Inside trimmed with roses. Ca. 1865.* **Value:** $125.00

Plate 115: *Inside view.*

Beginning in 1867, hats and bonnets both began to be worn tilted forward over the forehead. This was due mostly to accommodate a change in fashionable hairstyles. The bun or chignon most women wore at the back of the neck was now worn higher up.

The bonnet began to lose popularity to the hat in the 1870s. The most popular hat of the early 1870s was a high-crowned hat shaped much like a small version of a man's derby. These sometimes had turned-up brims which were filled with flowers. These high-crowned hats disappeared around 1875. The new hat for the second half of the decade had a lower crown and a medium brim which turned up at the back.

Hats and bonnets of the 1870s were generally more elaborately trimmed than in the 1860s. A common feature of the early 1870s hat was ribbons at the back which hung over the high chignon. These ribbons were not seen much after 1876. Flowers became a popular trim, "field flowers" being most popular as opposed to more formal garden flowers. Also in the second half of the 1870s, whole birds began to be used as trimmings.

The most popular hat of 1878 is the "Gainsborough," a round-crowned hat with a wide brim turned up at one side. This remained fashionable for most of the 1880s. The "Post Boy" hat, a very high-crowned hat with a narrow to no brim, which looked somewhat like an upside-down flowerpot was popular from 1884-1888. From 1877 to 1884, a brimless, helmet-shaped bonnet with wide strings was seen. (See Plate 116.)

After 1884, brims arched or turned up in points over the forehead (see Plate 117). In 1887, smaller bonnets were seen with low, flat crowns and strings situated far to the back. (See Plate 118.)

Plush, velvet, and felt were popular fabrics for hats and bonnets of the 1880s. Straw was seen for summer wear and around 1888, straw woven with alternating rows of velvet was popular for winter wear. Brims of straw hats and bonnets were often lined with velvet throughout the 1880s. Beaver fur hats were found after 1887.

Feathers were the most frequently used trimming in the 1880s. Small rodents, insects and even lizards were sometimes seen as trimmings in fashion periodicals of this time; however these trimmings rarely survive intact. Jet or glass beading was another popular trim and brims were sometimes edged with fringes of beads. Asymmetrical trimming on hats complimented the asymmetrical trimming of skirts in 1886-1888. From 1885, trimmings were often arranged in a point or arch at the front, keeping the illusion of height as the high-crowned hats began to diminish in size. Whole bird wings, stiffened bands of ribbon and standing feathers contributed to this effect.

Hats and bonnets of the 1890s are easily identified by one distinguishing feature which remains constant throughout the decade — a single high ornament (such as a feather, tuft of horsehair or stiffened ribbon) which protrudes above the rest of the trimming. (See Plates 119 and 121.)

Plate 116: *Helmet-shaped bonnet of velvet trimmed with beads and feathers. Satin ribbon ties. Ca. 1883.* **Value: $130.00**

Plate 117: *Small straw hat with cloth flowers and bead trim. Survives as part of a matching outfit. See Plate 35. Ca. 1885.*

From 1890 to 1894, the most popular form of head wear was the toque, a small, pancake-like, round, brimless hat. These were buried under mounds of trimmings and worn flat on the top of the head (see Plate 119). Toque- style bonnets were also popular, being distinguished by retaining ties which were now very narrow (less than one inch wide) and set well at the back (see Plate 120). By the mid-1890s, the bonnet with strings had become a strictly "middle-aged" fashion and by the end of the century, bonnets with strings were completely discarded.

A narrow, boat-shaped hat worn high on the head with narrow brims turned up was popular after 1893 and as hats begin increasing in height around 1895, hats with cone-shaped crowns were briefly seen.

Coarse or fancy plaited straw sailor hats with or without elaborate trimmings gained popularity during the 1890s and were worn with medium width brims and a flat crown. (See Plate 121.)

By 1897, larger hats with wide brims upturned on one side were worn high on the head (see Plate 113). By the last years of the century, hats were larger with soft full crowns and high trimmings.

In addition to materials popular in the 1880s, sequins, lace and chiffon were found in hat trimmings of the 1890s. Feathers and beads remained popular, although the effect was somewhat lighter than the 1880s. A typical 1890s trimming was fabric bunched together and sewn into shapes (see Plate 119). Ribbons and bows were stiffened with wire to stand straight up, and flowers abounded, with violets being especially the rage.

Beginning in 1900, hats were much larger than previously seen and gradually increased in size over the next few years (see Plate 51). Hats were worn straight on the head until around 1905 when an extreme tilt forward was most fashionable and many hats of this period had ornamental flowers or gathered bunches of material at the back to fill in the gap left between the underside of the brim and the head by this extreme tilt. (See Plate 122.)

By 1908 hats lost their tilt and once again rested straight on the head. These hats had wide crowns and large brims slanted downward, their crowns often completely covered with trimmings such as flowers, lace or feathers. Crowns became lower and wider, lying nearly flat against straight brims in 1909, giving a somewhat squashed appearance. (See Plate 123.)

Brims continued to increase in size (see Plate 124). By 1911, some very large hats measured over 2 yards in circumference. As hats grew larger, trimmings began to diminish. The very large hats were sometimes difficult to keep in place and these often had filaments of stiffened material inside the space between the crown and head that kept the hat in place.

The most popular trimming for hats in the early years of this century was ostrich plumes and feathers dyed to match the color of the hat. Velvet, plush and lace were also used and straw hats were still worn in summer. Fur and fur trimming were seen on winter hats.

Plate 118: *Small straw bonnet with black lace trim. Ca. 1887.* **Value: $45.00**

Plate 119: *Velvet toque trimmed with cloth flowers, sequins, beads, bunched velvet fabric, and single high standing feather. Ca. 1891.* **Value: $195.00**

Plate 120: *Toque-style bonnet with applique lace ties, cloth flowers and beaded trim. Ca. 1893.* **Value: $185.00**

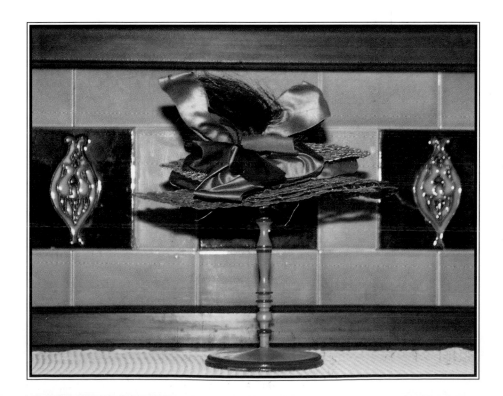

Plate 121: *Fancy plaited straw sailor hat with satin ribbon and tuft of horsehair. Ca. 1895.* **Value: $125.00**

Plate 122: *Velvet and straw hat with ostrich feather trim. The hat was worn tilted over the forehead. Ca. 1906.* **Value: $145.00**

Plate 123: *Lace hat with ostrich feather brim. Ca. 1909.* **Value: $95.00**

In 1912, large-crowned hats with wide brims, similar to though smaller in size and less trimmed than those previously worn, were popular. These continued to be worn until WWI when hats lost nearly all their trimmings and were made of practical materials. Close-fitting, turban-like hats and toques with high pointed or arched crowns in front were seen after 1912. By 1917, close-fitting hats with narrow, turned-up brims foreshadowed the cloches of the 1920s. Trimmings were limited to a single rosette or floral ornament center front or on one side. A single large ornament or ostrich plume standing straight up or cocked to one side was popular from 1912-1916. (See Plate 72.)

One of the most easily identified hat styles was the close fitting, helmet-shaped cloche which appeared around 1921. These were worn pulled down so far on the forehead that the eyebrows were hidden (see Plates 87 and 112). The first cloches were highly decorated and looser fitting (see Plate 125). By 1925, they were worn so tightly fitting that only women who bobbed their hair could wear them and trimming was limited to only one side in the late 1920s. (See Plates 126 and 127.)

The cloche continued in popularity into 1930 when it grew a small, narrow brim (see Plate 128). In the mid-1930s, this brim widened to frame the face (see Plates 129 and 130). Most hats of the remainder of the 1930s retained a round crown and medium brim. In addition, velvet was reintroduced in hats in 1930 after an absence of many years. These plush hats were helmet-shaped, but crushed onto the top of the head somewhat like a beret. Flatter hats shaped like pancakes and fitted onto a hairnet were introduced in 1936. These were followed by cartwheel-shaped hats in 1938 which foreshadowed the hats typical of the early 1940s.

Price Valuations

Elaborately trimmed hats and bonnets, 1850 – 1915	$95.00 – 200.00
Hats and bonnets with little trimming, 1850 – 1910	$20.00 – 125.00
Large hats with little trim, 1910 – 1920	$45.00 – 95.00
Cloche hats, 1920s	$25.00 – 95.00
Brimmed hats, 1930s	$20.00 – 45.00

Plate 124: *Large velvet hat with ostrich plumes. Ca. 1912.* **Value:** $175.00

Plate 125: *Flowered cloche hat. Ca. 1920.* **Value:** $25.00

Plate 126: *Straw cloche with satin ribbon. Ca. 1924.* **Value: $35.00**

Plate 127: *Black satin cloche with side tassel. Ca. 1926.* **Value: $30.00**

Plate 128: *Brimmed cloche with pheasant feathers. Ca. 1930.* **Value: $25.00**

Plate 129: *Petal-brimmed felt hat with curled feather. Ca. 1932.* **Value: $27.50**

Plate 130: *Brimmed felt hat with cloth gardenias. Ca. 1936.* **Value: $35.00**

1910

CHAPTER X
Parasols

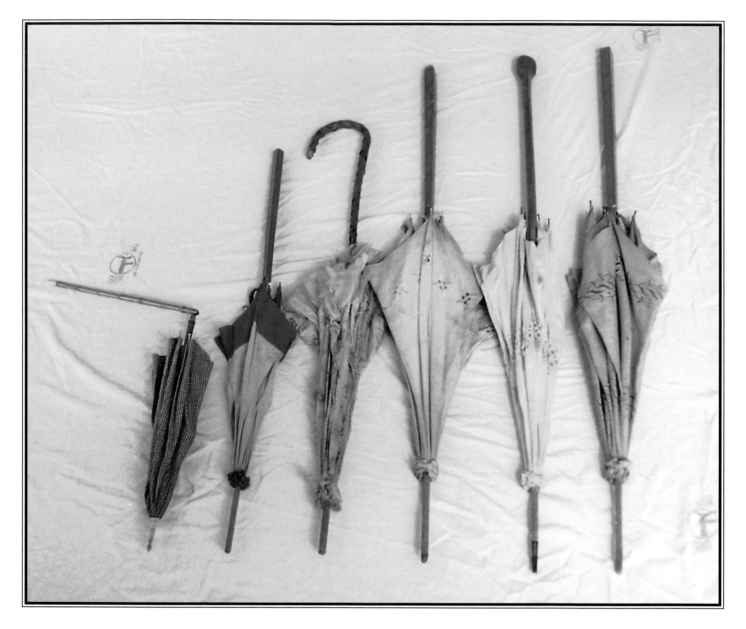

Plate 131: *The evolution of the parasol. From left to right: hinged parasol 1860s, 1870s, 1880s, 1890s, 1900s, 1910s.*

> *"The most useful and distinguished are undoubtedly the large parasols of black brocade bordered with deep real lace; but fashion does not now sanction black parasols with colored toilets, and it is incumbent upon ladies, therefore, to possess themselves of at least one of the new styles brocaded in colors."*
>
> **Demorest's Monthly Magazine**
> **May 1880**

Not merely a sunshade, the parasol was an important fashion accessory and purchased to match or complement a certain costume.

Early Victorian parasols were very small, and parasol lengths increased steadily into the next century, thus making parasols easy to date with the aid of a tape measure. Measurements are taken from tip of the "ferrule" (pointed or round tip above the cover) to the bottom of the handle.

Length of Parasol (from ferrule to handle)	Date
22 to 28 inches	1835-1865
25 to 30 inches	1865-1885
36 to 40 inches	1885-1899
40 to 42 inches	after 1900

Early parasols most often had a hinge in the stick which allowed them to fold in half for convenient storage. A tube of metal or ivory slid over this hinge when it was open (see Plates 131 and 133). They sometimes had an additional hinge which allowed the cover to tilt toward the direction of the sun. These sticks were very slender compared to later sticks. The most elegant had handles of ivory or coral which were worked in elaborate designs. Simpler handles were more common, made of turned wood with ivory ends. In 1851, metal frames with steel ribs began to be manufactured; however cane ribbing was less expensive and was found in many, plainer parasols at this time. Whalebone ribs were also seen on early parasols and these, along with cane ribs, were not seen after 1870.

By 1866, the parasol with the long slender, folding stick was outdated and replaced by a parasol which was shorter and had a thicker stick (see Plate 132). Carved heads of animals and birds decorated the handles of some parasols in the 1870s. An awning of deep lace was first seen beginning at this time.

The most popular parasols of the 1880s had knotty or gnarled wood handles or sticks (see Plate 134). Brightly colored insects sometimes decorated the handles in this decade.

A novelty of the 1880s was the Japanese paper parasol with a bamboo handle, popularized by Sarah Bernhardt when she carried one in 1881 on stage in *La Dame Aux Camelias* (see Plate 135). These parasols were fashionable throughout the 1880s and should not be confused with the much larger and longer Japanese-styled parasols found after 1910 or the cheaply made souvenir parasols still manufactured today.

Plate 132: *Wood handle, muslin cover. Ca. 1870s.* **Value: $100.00**

Plate 133: *Parasol with hinged, simulated bamboo wood handle, cane ribbing, cotton cover, ivory ferrule and rib tips. Ca. early 1860s.* **Value: $155.00**

Plate 134: *Gnarled wood handle with printed silk cover. Ca. 1880s.* **Value: $125.00**

Plate 135: *Japanese paper parasol with wood handle. Ca. 1885.* **Value: $65.00**

By 1885, parasols grew longer and appeared slimmer when closed. Parasols of the 1890s were generally plain and had large covers measuring up to 35 inches in diameter. They often had long pointed ferrules and doubled as walking sticks.

In 1896, attention was focused on the lining and for several years "geisha" parasols with plain covers and puffed chiffon or silk linings were popular.

Parasols at the turn of the century were as elaborate as dresses of the day. These were the parasols with lace inserts, or made completely of lace or transparent materials lined with colored fabrics. Handles were usually straight. (See Plate 136.)

Around 1904, parasols became plainer and more umbrella-like in appearance because they were used more as sunshades than as fashionable accessories (see Plate 137). By 1920, the parasol had fallen out of fashion except with older ladies who clung to their sunshades for a few more years. In 1922, an attempt to revive the parasol was made with the "canine parasol" which had a dog's head carved into the handle. This revived the parasol among dog lovers; however, the fashion was soon discarded.

Price valuations

Prices of parasols may vary greatly since some have real gems, carved ivory, gold or mother of pearl inlay on their sticks. These are relatively rare and the following price guide is based on the common parasol with a wood handle.

Parasols with elaborate or folding sticks	$75.00 – 225.00
Parasols with simple sticks	$60.00 – 125.00
Parasols with lace or silk coverings, elaborately trimmed	$95.00 – 175.00

Plate 136: *Muslin and lace covered parasol with wood handle. Ca. 1900.* **Value:** $115.00

Plate 137: *Embroidered cotton covered parasol with straight wood handle. Ca. 1910.* **Value:** $85.00

Chapter XI
Care and Restoration

Plate 138: *Cotton batiste shirtwaist, ca. 1905. Garment has many stains, lace insert tearing out.* **No value in this condition.**

Storage

Unfortunately, the most common place that old clothing is stored is in the attic. This is the worse place possible, as extremes in temperature will cause fibers to swell and contract which result in stress tears in fabrics. Collectors should keep their antique and vintage clothing stored in their living quarters where the climate is relatively controlled. In addition, do not store old fabric in wood trunks or paper boxes. Wood products are acidic to old fabric, and the acid can cause both staining and weakening of the fibers. Acid-free boxes and tissue papers are available and are the best means for storing old fabrics. However, the same effect can be achieved by wrapping the article in cotton sheets before storing in a wood trunk or dresser drawer. Make sure there is no bleach or starch in the sheets or the article itself since these may attract moths.

Never fold old fabric; the creases will eventually become weakened over the years and will tear. When possible, roll the article in a ball, or if you must fold the article, you should refold it twice a year so that the creases do not set.

Heavy articles should not be hung on hangers since the weight will cause tearing in the shoulder seams. Lighter articles can be hung on padded, fabric-covered hangers.

Cleaning and Restoration

If you have a historically significant article of clothing (i.e., associated with a historically significant person or event), please consult a museum curator before attempting any of the following methods. Museum curators have conservation techniques available to them which are not in the realm of the average collector.

DO NOT ATTEMPT to clean old velvet or any article that has become very fragile over the years. These articles are best cleaned by a professional dry cleaner who has experience with vintage fabrics.

Cottons and cotton blends are the most easily cleaned of any vintage fabrics. White cottons can be cleaned by washing in warm water with a gentle soap and a mild, non-chlorine bleach. If you are soaking difficult stains, be sure to change the water regularly. Letting the water cool will result in setting the stains deeper. Hair spray is also effective for removing stains on cotton. Spray the stain before washing. This process may have to be repeated several times before a stain will disappear. Stains on colored cottons can be removed this way also; however, spot test any colored fabric before immersing to make sure the dye will not run.

Other Household Stain Removers

White vinegar will remove some perspiration stains. Dab the vinegar on the stain before washing. It can also be brushed onto a perspiration stain on a non-washable fabric. Be careful not to oversaturate.

Lemon juice and salt will remove some rust stains. Lemon may discolor some fabrics, so spot test this in an inconspicuous place before applying.

Denatured alcohol will remove some dye stains. Sponge the stain with the alcohol in a circular motion, feathering the edges so a ring will not form.

Plate 139: *The type of stain easily removed with hair spray. See restored garment in Plate 59.*

Commercial Stain Removers

I have had varying luck with commercial stain removers. Many are too toxic for old fabrics. Test them on an inconspicuous spot before you use them. The dry stick stain removers are the gentlest; they are available in chalk form and can be used on all fabrics.

Dyeing

Often stains that have set too long are simply unremovable. If stains are light and fabric is light colored, dyeing is an alternative. This can be done with regular, over the counter dyes but must be done by the hand method, not with a washing machine. This can be tedious, but the results are well worth it. The 1926 dress in Plate 92 is an example of a dress that has been dyed to cover the stains. It was originally white and had light yellow stains that were unremovable. Be sure to use a color that is appropriate to the vintage of the dress.

Rips and Tears

Rips and tears can be mended but should be mended by hand. Any sewing should take place before washing or dyeing the fabric. If you are dyeing a fabric, use a color of thread for mending that matches the new color, not the old.

Tears that are not in seams can sometimes be camouflaged by sewing a small pleat or dart over them. Make a corresponding pleat or dart on the other side of the garment, if possible, so that the repair is not so noticeable.

Pressing and Ironing

Steaming is the gentlest method for pressing old fabrics and handheld steamers can be purchased at reasonable costs. Do not iron velvet which will crush the pile. If you must iron velvet, iron on the reverse side on a moderate setting. Better yet, take it to a professional cleaner and have it steam-pressed.

Starching can be done if the clothing is to be worn or displayed immediately. Do not store starched fabric since it attracts moths.

In closing, if an article of clothing is stained or torn beyond repair, remember that many doll collectors and crafts people will pay fair prices for vintage fabrics to be remade into doll clothes or crafts. Clothing in disrepair is also valuable to the makers of reproduction clothing and reproduction textiles.

Plate 140. *After restoration: restored cotton batiste shirtwaist. Stains removed, lace insert resewn by hand. Damaged piece shown Plate 138.* **Value after restoration: $85.00.**

Photo Quiz

Can you date these photographs by the fashions that are worn? Answers are on page 125.

A.

B.

C.

D.

E.

F.

Photograph Quiz answers: A. 1911 B. 1887
C. 1904 D. 1926 E. 1923 F. 1918